THE BREAKTHROUGH STRATEGY

THE BREAKTHROUGH STRATEGY

Using Short-term Successes to Build the High Performance Organization

ROBERT H. SCHAFFER

BALLINGER PUBLISHING COMPANY
Cambridge, Massachusetts
A Subsidiary of Harper & Row, Publishers, Inc.

International Standard Book Number: 0-88730-276-9

Library of Congress Catalog Card Number: 88-19247

Printed in the United States of America

LIBRARY OF CONGRESS
Library of Congress Cataloging-in-Publication Data

Schaffer, Robert H.
  The breakthrough strategy.
  ISBN 0-88730-2767-9
  1. Organizational change. 2. Organizational effectiveness. I. Title.
HD58.8.S297   1988   658.4′063   88-19247

>> Contents

Acknowledgements   vii

Chapter 1
  The Hidden Reserve   1

Part I   The Quest to Be Competitive

Chapter 2
  Built-in Barriers to Performance Improvement   18

Chapter 3
  Perpetual Preparations Waste Billions   39

**Part II   The Breakthrough Strategy: Success as the Building
           Block**

Chapter 4
  The Zest Factors Reveal What's Possible   52

Chapter 5
Design Each Project for Certain Success   61

Chapter 6
Use Each Success to Develop Performance Capability   76

Chapter 7
Widening the Circle of Success   94

Part III   Breakthrough Projects: Vehicles for Innovation

Chapter 8
From Proselytizers to Allies: A Shifting Role for
Staff Specialists   114

Chapter 9
Tactics for Mastering Strategy   128

Chapter 10
Management Development Through Management
Achievement   144

Chapter 11
Quality Improvement by Improving Quality   162

Part IV   The High-Performance, Change-Oriented Organization

Chapter 12
Putting It All Together   178

About the Author   195

>> *Acknowledgements*

The breakthrough strategy, both as a concept and as a practical set of working procedures, has developed over many years through application and refinement by a number of colleagues working together. I want to acknowledge the importance of this collaboration in the development of the strategy—and to thank specifically those associates whose projects are represented in the book: Ronald Ashkenas, Richard Bobbe, Grant Davies, Claude Guay, Robert Neiman, Rudi Siddik, Peter Sindell, Martin Strasmore, and Harvey Thomson. I should also recognize the contributions of Anton Pritchard and the late Phillip Woodyatt, with whom I first formulated the basic ideas many years ago.

Keith Michaelson gathered and developed the case materials and provided valuable assistance in the editing of the manuscript.

Barbara Smalter did yeoman work in processing the manuscript through its evolving stages; Emilieanne Koehnlein assisted, especially with the graphics; and Ruth Dearborn provided the overall support and coordination that made it possible for the writing and word processing to get done in the face of many other competing pressures.

Finally, we want to recognize the contributions of the many managers—both those mentioned in the book and others—who have employed the breakthrough strategy in accelerating the performance of their organizations. Their willingness to venture, to commit, and to experiment has continuously enriched the breakthrough concept and has provided many demonstrations of how much more organizations are really capable of achieving.

1

>> *The Hidden Reserve*

On a Friday afternoon the Industrial Paints Division of PPG Industries received a call from a company they had long sought as a customer. The company was running out of a highly specialized paint product and urgently needed a shipment by Monday. Their regular supplier could not guarantee delivery. Could PPG deliver on such short notice?

At the time, Industrial Paints was running at full capacity— seven days, three shifts. It usually took at least several weeks of careful planning to formulate a special order in the lab and then introduce it into the production schedule. But this was a rare opportunity. They promised delivery for Monday.

The task was formidable: the chemists had to develop and test the product, then specify the formulation process. Production had to find the needed facilities; Shipping had to organize the transportation.

On Sunday afternoon, the shipment was on its way to the customer. No ongoing production was delayed.

Almost every manager I've ever talked with can match that story with tales of similar "miracles" in their own companies. They can also tell you what happens once the urgency disappears. The superior performance disappears with it. Life goes back to normal, and managers who have witnessed people perform at levels that far exceeded their normal output, quickly forget that the heroic efforts ever happened.

In this widely shared experience, there is a powerful clue as to why companies have had such difficulty meeting tough competitive challenges—and also a clue as to what they can do differently. During the past twenty-five years, I have devoted my professional life to uncovering the mystery of why, in "normal" times, individuals and organizations always look and feel busy—even overworked and harassed—but are able to double, triple, and even quadruple their output when the situation requires them to do so.

The key is that during normal times, in most organizations, unbelievably vast quantities of potentially productive capacity are untapped, undemanded, unused or frittered away. This great store of "hidden reserve" is what we observe when organizations rise to meet crisis situations. This insight is the foundation for the "breakthrough strategy," a strategy that has enabled many different kinds of organizations to tap into their hidden reserves to produce major performance gains.

❯❯ *A Tale of Two Companies*

The corporate offices of Greyline Telecommunications set the scene: the heavy wooden furniture and framed photographs call to mind the early years of the telecommunications industry. People move about with decorum and speak to each other in hushed voices, much as they would in a library.

Greyline managers consider their company successful. Compared with the Bell System companies in the United States, its performance ranks at about the midpoint. Any Greyline manager whose unit is performing comparably to the Bell System average is, in fact, considered to be doing "all right."

Each year, Greyline managers forecast their operating expenses and capital expenditures; these requirements are then translated into rate increase requests made to the government's rate regulators. While Greyline prides itself on being competently managed and up-to-date technically, there is no strong drive to become more productive or, in fact, to change very much in any way.

Greyline owns a subsidiary that makes its telecommunications equipment. Not really viewed as a separate business, the subsidiary exists mainly to supply the parent. It does its job relatively well, but shows little drive to innovate or improve. Performance shortcomings or user complaints are usually dealt with by task forces that spend many months analyzing and discussing.

Let's compare Greyline with another company—one that used to be a telephone company but is now one of the largest conglomerates in Canada: Bell Canada Enterprises (BCE). BCE's subsidiary, Bell Canada, is still in telecommunications, but that is only one of the many related businesses that now make up the company, which is also involved in international telecommunications consulting, energy, publishing, and packaging. Bell Canada could not be more different from Greyline. For many years, it has been an industry leader in productivity, cost, and service.

Like Greyline, BCE also has a major stake in a telecommunications manufacturer, the well-known Northern Telecom. That company entered the U.S. market around 1980 and within a few years had outpaced every other manufacturer—including GTE, ITT, Stromberg-Carlson, and Siemens—to become second only to AT&T. Northern Telecom is one of the few North American suppliers to Nippon Telephone and Telegraph, which is about the most sophisticated buyer of electronic equipment in the world.

When books are written about the weak competitive ability of North American industry, the finger is pointed at companies like old Greyline to explain our deplorable condition. Companies like BCE are extolled as the symbols of what might be possible.

But Greyline and BCE are the same company. "Greyline" is Bell Canada before its transformation—a transformation that started not with fantasies of world conquest, nor with a long-range planning study, nor with a "culture change program," nor with a quest for magical, new managerial styles. This transformation began with disciplined, determined efforts to improve the most fundamental aspects of the company's operations: the way work was done at its basic levels, and the way changes were carried out. The company began by increasing the competence of its managers to make things happen faster, to improve fundamental operations. "Greyline" began its transformation by creating expectations throughout the company that constant improvement would become a way of life.

Making Miracles Routine

This book will show that almost every organization has the capacity to make similar changes. It will illustrate the strategy that many corporations (as well as governments, health care groups, and other organizations) have used to achieve such changes. It will describe how these companies began: not by jumping on the magic carpet of the latest managerial fad, in the hope of being whisked to the promised land of treasure and success, but by using familiar ideas and concepts. Often disdained as merely the "management basics," these ideas helped them tap into their hidden reserves and achieve their transformations. In every case, progress started not with high drama, secret formulas, or bold strokes, but with the accomplishment of urgently needed improvements in current performance.

Every manager who has become disenchanted with the search for the "right" magic answer to the dilemma of increasing competitiveness, and who is ready to roll up his or her sleeves and get to work, will find here an exciting and readily applicable methodology.

›› *Our Slow Response to a Rude Awakening*

In the 1960s American industrial managers were reluctant to admit that their long-standing world preeminence was being threatened. Since the early 1970s, however, the shock waves of rising foreign competition have inundated one industry after the next. The automotive and steel industries, consumer electronics and machine tools, and dozens of others have been rocked by the emergence of low-cost, high-quality imports.

Managers gradually found it necessary to face up to the need for major improvements in performance, and billions of dollars have been invested in the effort. Some has been spent on new plant and equipment and on automation, some on the development of products and new processes. Enormous energy has been expended in the search for new management styles, techniques, and methodologies that will make our corporations more effective. Although there has been some progress, there is no evidence yet, despite all these efforts, that the tide is really turning.

Many managers have begun to wonder: Is this the best we can do? What's wrong? With all the investment we have been making and all the good advice we have been receiving, must the results continue to be so disappointing? My answer is a firm no.

The Potential Is There

While many performance-limiting patterns are deeply embedded in our companies, plenty of evidence suggests that the decline of industry has not been an inevitable consequence of the American work ethic or cultural patterns. For example, after unsuccessful domestic producers sold or closed plants, Japanese firms have moved in and revitalized the facilities. More than 500 Japanese companies are now manufacturing or assembling their products in the United States. In the well-publicized GM-Toyota joint venture, NUMMI, Toyota is assembling high-quality, low-cost cars in a plant that had been abandoned by GM. Toyota hired back the old GM work force and, with little investment in new technology, has achieved better results than most of GM's new plants.

A number of American companies—such as Motorola and Northern Telecom, who sell their products in Japan, and Harley-Davidson, recently resuscitated from near death—have made dramatic breakthroughs in performance, rivaling the best of the Japanese companies. While their numbers are small, they prove that world-class competitive performance can be achieved by American companies. The fuel to energize transformation lies right within every organization—in the hidden reserve of unused or misused capability that is "miraculously" revealed in crises.

A Walkout Shows What's Possible

Many years ago, at the Bayway Refinery of Exxon (then Esso), I first recognized the significance of this sudden, dramatic rise in output generated by a crisis. As a young consultant, I was assigned to interview a number of the refinery's supervisors and managers.

To lower costs, this Linden, New Jersey refinery had just recently reduced its work force from 3,000 people to about 2,700. The reduction was a shock. Supervisors insisted that top management had "gone too far," and that they would not be able to maintain traditional quality, service, and safety levels with the reduced force.

At the time, a jurisdictional dispute existed between two factions of workers who wanted different unions. The conflict intensified until a spontaneous work stoppage occurred. It began on one unit; over the next several days, workers on other units began to walk off their jobs. Assuming that the demonstration would be over shortly, supervisors and engineers stepped into unfamiliar roles and kept the units running. Within a few days, however, *all* of the hourly employees were on the outside, and the plant was being run by about 450 supervisors, managers, and engineers.

This makeshift team had to postpone major maintenance projects, of course, but they ran the refinery well. They ran it safely. They delivered product "on spec" and on time. And they did it not just for a few days, but for four months.

This was all rather astonishing to the young management consultant who had gone to the refinery to do some fact-finding interviews. There was no disputing the intensity and the sincerity of the prestrike complaints about the inadequacy of having only 2,700 people to run the refinery—but then I saw it being run by a small fraction of that number. What's more, the people who ran it, instead of feeling resentment at being overworked, actually seemed to feel a special sense of drama and excitement, which they had never experienced in the organization before. It was an adventure, a challenge, and they talked about their feat for years after.

The Possibilities Are Limitless

Managers are often skeptical when we use examples like PPG's Industrial Paints and Bayway to suggest that vast reservoirs of untapped and unused capability exist in their own organizations. They protest in several ways:

> "Wait a minute. Maybe people can work at these fantastic rates for a little while—but not indefinitely. You'd have burnout throughout your operations."

> "Yes—moreover, you don't want to be running your organization in a crisis atmosphere all the time."

> "Sure, and in crisis situations, people concentrate on one thing and let other things drop. Anyone can do that."

> "These big gains may be possible in inefficient companies, but we run a very tight ship. You could never do anything like that in my company."

If you share these doubts, you have plenty of company. I urge you to set your skepticism aside, at least temporarily, and allow yourself to see how you might be able to tap into the most readily available resource for major gains in competitiveness—unused, unsuspected, or dissipated capability, which you are paying for anyway, though you are not getting much in return. You'll have to set aside the assumption that your company—or at least the part that you manage—is operating close to its maximum capacity, given the available resources and people.

The breakthrough strategy begins with quite different beliefs and assumptions. Join me in testing the view that most companies are functioning at only 40, 50, or 60 percent of their capacity, and that the much higher levels of performance reached in emergencies—when a major new customer might be brought in, when a new product must be developed in record time, when a natural disaster strikes, when the employees walk out—are actually much closer to true, sustainable potentials than are the "normal" levels of performance.

If you consider that those crisis performance levels are *spontaneously* generated with a minimum of formal organization and technological or management systems innovations, you can begin to imagine how much might be possible if the crisis-motivated forces were combined with sophisticated, managed

improvement. The breakthrough strategy applies the beneficial
lessons of crisis situations in ways that not only make the company more competitive, but also make it a more rewarding, gratifying, and humane place to work.

When managers who believe they are pushing the limits
of what can be achieved are asked to produce improvements,
they naturally think at once of adding resources: new equipment, new systems, better measurements, additional training,
new people, or more support from other functions. Starting with
the 40–60 percent of actual capacity assumption, the breakthrough strategy aims at getting better performance right away,
from the underemployed resources at hand. This focus on immediate results is the central concept underlying the breakthrough
strategy. It is sometimes difficult for people to accept—so brain-
washed have we become into looking outside of ourselves for
the keys to improvement.

» *Down the Garden Path of Emulation*

As companies have fallen further behind, managers have
searched intensively for an antidote. A flood of books, studies,
and packaged programs claim to provide the "right answers."
While varying considerably in emphasis and point of view, these
studies share a single method. They all select outstanding companies in Japan or North America and then scrutinize them to
identify the factors that seem to have made them successful.
Those factors are then set forth as the model to be emulated.
Some of these models focus on management style or employee
relations, others emphasize business strategy or manufacturing
methods. Still others describe more complex combinations of
success factors.

This approach to formulating an improvement strategy
might seem quite logical; and yet it is fatally flawed. There is
a joke about the leader of a poor country who discovered that
the people in the world's richest countries owned many more
television sets, per capita, than his own people. He concluded
that he should provide his people with television sets, as the

basis for future prosperity. We may chuckle at his naivete—but how different is his logic from that of a company that spends millions of dollars providing its people with quality control training programs, because employee concern for quality is prevalent in Japan's most successful companies? The particular factors noticed by outside observers studying successful companies may not be the factors that enabled those companies to achieve their success in the first place.

There is a second, more serious flaw in this "emulate the winners" approach. Even if we could identify the critical factors that made IBM, Hewlett-Packard, Northern Telecom, or any of the best Japanese companies successful, there is no evidence that even strenuous efforts by a company to transfuse these individual elements into itself would make it successful. Its cultural, structural, and psychological patterns may be fundamentally different from those of its succcessful model; thus, the policies and programs that worked so well for the model company may do little for the emulating company. The notion that one can lift the features of one company, graft them onto another, and produce the same results, simply has little basis in fact.

We smile when we see a beginning skier spare no expense to purchase the same kind of skis worn by Olympic champions, or when the duffer, under the illusion that they will really make a difference in his game, shows up on the golf course with the most expensive woods. We know that becoming an expert in golf or skiing is an arduous process of hard work and gradual development. Acquiring the gestures, styles, or equipment of an expert has never enabled anyone to circumvent that process.

Making a company successful, effective, and capable of rapid change is a difficult and comprehensive developmental process. Most of the advice available to management pays scant attention to this developmental process and rarely shows how companies can deliberately evolve from being less to more competitive over time. Rather, it paints a picture of someone else's end result as the ideal; managers are told to take a deep breath, gather their resolve, and then make their companies "be like that."

Strategy as the False Idol

Of all the areas where the ideal has been extolled as the only model, none has created as much managerial discomfort and off-target behavior as the call for more strategic planning. In searching to discover "what hit us," many theorists ascribe the erosion in the American competitive position to the shortsightedness of management. If only American managers could take the strategic view, could anticipate what is coming and plan accordingly—with the same vision and perseverance as the best of the Japanese—American industry's salvation would be at hand.

Underlying this message has been a steady drumbeat of accusation: "American managers are too preoccupied with the next quarter's results." "No wonder the Japanese companies have been eating our lunch; they anticipate long-term market trends and then spend whatever it takes to penetrate the markets they've selected."

Managers have internalized the belief that if they could somehow come up with the right strategic plan, they too could be successful. The spectacular growth of the strategy consulting industry is but one piece of evidence that the message has hit home. While many companies have undoubtedly benefited from better strategic planning, in many more the planning efforts made no difference in their ability to compete. The automobile industry is an obvious example: by 1980, American automobile executives had certainly figured out what was happening to their industry and had generated plenty of good strategic responses. The Big Three companies pursued major new strategic directions; they invested more than $40 billion in automated manufacturing and were struggling to produce a competitive small car. What were the results? Not all that great. Costs remained higher than those of the Japanese, and their domestically manufactured small cars did little to slow the pace of imports.

What happened in the automobile industry, as well as in many others, was that the expected benefits of good strategies were thwarted by limitations in their ability to carry out innovation. When a company adopts "long-range planning" without significantly improving its ability to make things happen, success is unlikely.

❯❯ *Overlooking Basic Performance Capability*

In their preoccupation with strategic vision, with bold marketing thrusts, with plans for large-scale automation, American managers have missed a fundamental point, and we are paying a tremendous price for this error. In all the attempts to "emulate the winner," senior managers have bypassed the task of strengthening the basic capacity of the organization and its people to get their jobs done much more rapidly and effectively.

Compare these two companies: In Company A, a customer with a complaint calls a salesperson, who takes the information and writes a memo to his boss, the district manager. The district manager passes the memo on to Customer Service. After sitting in Customer Service for a few days, the memo moves on to Engineering. Several weeks later, the customer receives a letter explaining that there have been virtually no other complaints of the type that he has raised. The letter suggests that he may be using the product incorrectly.

In Company B, the same complaint sparks a number of phone calls by the salesperson and her boss, who organizes a brief meeting with Customer Service and Engineering. That same day, an engineer is on the phone with the customer, working on the problem. When the customer is asked to return the product for repair, Customer Service makes sure that a substitute is delivered to him, and that the repair turnaround is speedy. As soon as a few similar problems occur with any prodcut, Company B makes changes in the product's design or manufacture.

Multiply these differences between Company A and Company B by 100, by 1000, or by 10,000. This is the difference between the highly productive, responsive companies and the laggards. No matter what else they may have done along the way, every successful company has developed the work patterns and habits, the attitudes and relationships, the policies and procedures, and the skills and the experience to guarantee that thousands of basic tasks are done well, are done rapidly, and are customer-responsive.

Most managements have largely failed to comprehend that basic performance capacity is the absolute weakest link in our struggle to be competitive. While American companies search far and wide for ever more esoteric formulas to get them back into the running, some very powerful solutions lie close at hand. The starting point for a turnaround is not strategic visions, nor automation, nor "total quality programs," nor Japanese manufacturing approaches—although every one of these may contribute greatly to the solution.

While basic performance capability can be improved best through a deliberate, managed, step-by-step process, this book will show you how to accelerate this learning process. The following example will provide a brief preview of the approach.

>> *A Sweet Story of Success at Amstar*

In 1982, Amstar Corporation, maker of Domino Sugar, was the victim of fate. The rising use of sugar substitutes was reducing the size of its market, while the government was keeping the cost of imported raw cane sugar high to protect domestic beet and corn sugar producers. Amstar had to find a way to reduce costs significantly, or they would continue to lose market share to competitors.

Only limited funds were available for new capital investment. In addition, the company's engineering programs and investments in new equipment during the previous years had not provided the needed performance improvements. Management was convinced that more had to be accomplished with the resources already in place.

The work began in Amstar's Baltimore refinery, where the manager, Frank Stowe, was ready to try something new. Stowe himself was keenly aware of what happens to companies that do not respond to the changing marketplace. His drive to work took him past many old factories standing idle near the Baltimore harbor, their windows broken and their gates locked. Signs of life emerged from the landscape only when he reached his sixty-year-old refinery, where 400 people were employed.

All of the refinery's departments needed improvement, but trying to tackle everything at once would be an overwhelming task. Instead, Stowe chose to focus on the packaging area, where refined sugar was packaged in 5-pound to 100-pound paper bags. Much sugar was being lost when bags were overfilled or broke while being filled. Given these conditions, how could the Baltimore refinery keep up with the competition?

The first project included only the one supervisor and seven hourly employees who operated the smallest packaging line. With the backing of local union leaders, this pilot team undertook the assignment to reduce overfill and spillage on their line. The project was launched with several informal work sessions with the team, not with elaborate training programs. The team set a few specific short-term goals and agreed on some ways to try to achieve them: making adjustments to the weighing scales; identifying damaged bags before they had a chance to break; resolving the unique packaging problems being caused by one particular grade of sugar. Within six weeks, the team had reached its first-step goals and by the end of three months, had reduced bag breakage by 80 percent and overfill by 56 percent.

Stowe expanded the process to other packaging lines and then, over the next several years, to every department in the refinery. In Chapter 7, I will come back to this story and describe how this first success led to very far-reaching improvements at the Baltimore refinery and at a second Amstar refinery in Chalmette, Louisiana.

The Amstar managers learned not only how to achieve significant, immediate results but also how to develop new work patterns that enabled them to use their initial successes as stepping stones to sustained improvement. So long as the managers had felt that they were doing everything they could and that help had to come from somewhere else, there was little hope for change. The critical shift occurred only when the managers learned how to produce better results—with the very same resources.

❯❯ *Start Small—Win Big*

The breakthrough strategy consists of locating and starting at once with the gains that can be achieved quickly, and then using those first successes as stepping stones to increasingly ambitious gains.

Detailed case illustrations in this book will show how the motivating, focusing, and energizing forces that stimulate heightened output during crises can be consciously incorporated into the life of an organization. I will describe in detail how you can expand your company's performance capability and how, as part of the process, you can much more effectively exploit innovations in technology and systems. The examples will show how the strategy has worked in electronics, transportation, chemicals, financial services, and many other kinds of companies, across the entire spectrum of operating and staff functions.

Part I begins by describing how the vice-like grip of psychological patterns and managerial norms keeps performance at abysmally low levels. It goes on to demonstrate why it is more valid to assume that companies are operating at 40–50 percent rather than close to capacity. Chapter 3 explains why so many of the programs and preparations in which companies are investing fail to fulfill their promise, even though they are technically sound.

Part II identifies the forces that are unleashed during performance-improving crises and explores why these forces are powerful enough to overcome institutionalized barriers. These forces can be exploited deliberately in breakthrough projects, without waiting for the next business crisis.

Part II also outlines how to make near-term, measurable results a virtual certainty, as well as how to incorporate the skills and disciplines needed for bolder gains. The initial successes can be multiplied into a widening circle of performance improvement, as I will illustrate in Chapter 7 with a number of actual cases.

Part III shows how the results-focused breakthrough projects provide opportunties for introducing new management methods, new technologies, and new tools and systems into companies. Instead of transfusing these innovations into organizations that are not capable of exploiting them, companies can introduce them gradually to support bottom-line achievements. Chapter 8 describes how internal staff specialists can ally themselves with user managers in a spirit of active collaboration. The subsequent chapters show how strategic planning, management development, and quality improvement can all contribute significantly to corporate progress if they are linked to the achievement of specific, short-term measurable goals.

Finally, in Chapter 12, you will see how top management can use the small, tangible steps of the initial performance breakthroughs, combined with strategic breakthroughs, to create not only organization-wide performance improvement but also a change-acceleration process that expands every aspect of competitive power. This comprehensive model will be contrasted with the "change the culture" programs based on the illusory hope that somehow, some way, success will follow. A detailed case will show how one business turned itself from a "cash cow" into a dynamic competitor.

So put your incredulity on hold for now. If you are willing to suspend your conviction that your company—or your part of the company—is close to or at the limits of its performance capacity, and accept that it may be functioning at a level far, far below what it could achieve, you may discover some powerful ways to improve performance and to accelerate innovation. You'll see that no matter how sophisticated your technologies may be, you have to focus first on the fundamentals of management—which hold the keys to breakthrough achievement.

>> PART I

The Quest to Be Competitive

2

>> Built-in Barriers to Performance Improvement

Can you remember ever hearing the president of an American company suggest that poor results were caused by his own leadership limitations? Did you ever hear the head of a manufacturing plant explain that defects in quality must be attributable to his own management approach? Did you ever hear the leader of a new product development team ascribe missed target dates to the way he ran the project? No. The president explains, "We have good products, but our advertising program did not seem to bring out the customers." The plant manager says, "We have been asking for new component test machines for months." And the project leader is sure that "we would have made the deadline, but two of our vendors held us up for parts."

All human behavior is a fascinating blend of the rational and the irrational, the conscious and the unconscious. We all like to believe that we perceive reality clearly, make logical judgments, and act in ways calculated to achieve our aims. That belief is partly true; at the same time, we tend to minimize anxiety by perceiving events and patterning our interactions with other people in ways that are least likely to raise tension or threaten our self-image. The slight bending of reality by the president, the plant manager, and the project leader, to avoid bruising their self-esteem, occurs over and over every day. They do it, and so does everyone they encounter.

This subtle behavior pattern is just one of the many unseen dynamics that can drag an organization down and slow its progress. When senior managers are searching for explanations for inadequate progress, they reach conclusions like: "Our people are resistant to change," or, "We have too many old managers set in their ways," or, "Our people don't really understand the seriousness of the situation. We need to get the message out." Most of these explanations describe merely the smallest tip of the iceberg. But it's hard to see below the surface because defensive behaviors mesh with management practices, organization habits, and company policies and procedures, forming barriers that inhibit, scatter, and dissipate the corporate resources.

❯❯ Built-in Barriers to Performance Improvement

❯ **Barrier 1: Psychological Myopia**
The tendency to view the world in ways that are psychologically comfortable and personally reassuring

❯ **Barrier 2: Wasteful Work Patterns**
The tendency to shape one's activities so as to stay busy with familiar routines and avoid anxiety-provoking challenges

❯ **Barrier 3: Weak Performance Expectations**
Avoiding risk by asking subordinates for less than is really possible or permitting them to escape from real commitments and consequences

❯ **Barrier 4: Misuse of Work Management Disciplines**
The tendency to be casual, careless, or cynical about work planning, measurement, and tracking procedures

❯ **Barrier 5: Invisible Conspiracy: The Underside of Corporate Culture**
The unique tangle of debilitating patterns that are reinforced by formal and informal institutional mechanisms

Before we can overcome such barriers, we need to understand how they became entrenched and how they reinforce each other. Because each organization is unique, it will be useful if you test the points below against your own situation. Start by identifying a unit in your organization whose performance you have some responsibility for. Then think about whether the barriers described here are at work in that unit.

» Barrier 1: Psychological Myopia

Observing managers in your own company, you'll see how often they explain that performance shortfalls or limitations are caused by factors outside of themselves. Almost every one of us imposes this critical warp on reality.

"Gimme More, Gimme More, Gimme More"

When they are asked to get more accomplished, to produce better quality, to achieve faster turnaround, more output or lower costs, managers not only will almost always point to external factors but will rarely see that they might achieve the results by managing more effectively.

In order to reduce inventories, materials managers say they need better forecasts from the field, more reliable deliveries from suppliers, fewer quality problems with incoming parts, and a better inventory control system. Salespeople will tell you that to increase sales they need more competitive products, better promotional material, more training, more exciting advertising, and, of course, more competitive pricing.

Denial

I will never forget a conversation some years ago with the president of a company that manufactured paperboard containers for ice cream. The company was borrowing heavily to build a large, new facility to produce more paperboard. At that time, plastic containers for ice cream were coming into vogue; I asked the president if he was concerned about that. Unable or unwilling to deal with this threatening development, he reached into his desk and pulled out a sample of one of his paper containers.

Displaying it fondly, he said, as much to reassure himself as to convince his listener, " You are never going to have a picture that looks so much like peach ice cream on a plastic container." The facility was built, and the company was in serious difficulties a few years later when demand had declined.

When reality is too painful, many managers find it easier to see things through rose-colored (or perhaps peach-colored) glasses, and they convince themselves that the plans or systems already in place will be adequate. Automobile manufacturers wouldn't believe that small cars were here to stay. IBM wouldn't believe that minicomputers—and later, personal computers—should be taken seriously. The sales manager won't believe that his best customer would switch to a competitor. The department manager won't believe that a favored subordinate is not capable of doing the job.

Faith in the Passage of Time

The president of a retail chain that was not doing very well showed me some figures he had put down on a pad. One of his competitors had just gone out of business, providing a boost to his own business. He had worked out the effect on his company if one or two more competitors went out of business. This company president was talking himself into believing that if he kept operating as he had been, sooner or later the bankruptcy of competitors would be his salvation.

Managers who are reluctant to change direction often rationalize that the passage of time will work in their favor. Reluctance to downsize when the market shrinks, for example, is explained away with, "This won't last long." The product manager with too much inventory asserts that rising sales in the next season will reduce the inventory to acceptable levels. When product quality is poor, the quality control manager reminds us that the product is on the early part of the learning curve and that, as experience is gained, quality is bound to improve.

There are dozens of other ways in which psychological myopia warps our view of what is going on. This myopia makes other people's performance look incompetent and our own, defensible.

Using the situation in your own organization that you identified earlier, turn to Diagnostic Work Sheet 2–1 and see whether psychological myopia may be one of the factors holding back the managers responsible for producing the needed results.

DIAGNOSTIC WORK SHEET 2–1

» *Psychological Myopia*

Organization _____

Improvement Needed _____

To what extent is progress toward this goal being slowed down by psychological myopia? Rate each statement according to how accurately it describes the actions of managers responsible for the goal.

	A Great Deal	Somewhat	Not Much (or Not at All)
The managers: Feel they're doing all they can; and that improvement depends on other groups or better resources	_____	_____	_____
Are denying or distorting some dimensions of reality	_____	_____	_____
Are assuming that time and changing conditions will cure the problem	_____	_____	_____
Resort to other kinds of rationalization (Name them)			
_____	_____	_____	_____
_____	_____	_____	_____
_____	_____	_____	_____

» *Barrier 2: Wasteful Work Patterns*

Many hours each week are taken up by regular meetings and chores over which a manager may have little control. How do managers allocate the remaining, very limited discretionary time? Henry Mintzberg points out that

> study after study has shown that managers' . . . activities are characterized by brevity, variety and discontinuity, and that [managers] are strongly oriented to action and dislike reflective activities. No study has found important patterns in the way managers schedule their time. They seem to jump from issue to issue, continually responding to the needs of the moment.[1]

My own observations confirm this pattern. Managers know how to make schedules, but they may lack a clear sense of how they should change their use of time to achieve better results. Just pondering this question can arouse uncertainty or uneasiness. It is much less anxiety-provoking to fill the day by responding to all the attention-grabbers—and by performing familiar and comfortable tasks. We all have our favorite activities that permit us to avoid the tough, complex managerial issues.

Busyness and Clinging to Routines

One of the most common ways that managers minimize anxiety is to simply keep busy. This busyness takes hundreds of forms: going for coffee or going to the bathroom; attending meetings at which your presence is not necessary; rushing out to the site of a crisis to gather data personally, when the information is available in other ways; closely supervising the work of subordinates, or jumping in to do their jobs for them.

Managers who get uneasy may rush off to do brief errands in the middle of meetings. Some managers take telephone calls during meetings, making the excuse, "This one I really have to take now." The typical "Mintzberg manager" rushing from meeting to meeting, from task to task, from telephone conversation to telephone conversation never has the time to stop and consider what it's all about. Am I making the best use of my time? What are the most important things I should be working on? Such questions can be disquieting. Bringing home an attache

---

1. Henry Mintzberg, "The Manager's Job: Folklore and Fact," *Harvard Business Review* (July–August 1975):50.

case full of correspondence and memoranda makes it equally unlikely that these uncertainties will haunt this manager's evenings.

Each of us develops certain habits that gradually become firmly embedded in our work life. One plant manager we know walks through his plant first thing every morning, stopping to talk to the people. He says he does it to keep in touch with what is happening on the shop floor. He feels a familiar sense of mastery and control as he walks along, chatting with people, solving the same old familiar problems. It is comforting and reassuring. But what else could he be doing with that time?

We all develop internalized patterns and routines that we perform automatically, all the while allowing ourselves to be distracted from completing other more complex and significant tasks. We also gradually build these patterns into the life of the organizations we manage.

At exactly noon every day, in a large chemical plant, fifteen or twenty managers meet in the superintendent's office to review current operations. They present reports, discuss problems, and share news. The meeting lasts an hour. Participants joke about the meeting as a way to "get in out of the rain;" privately, they say that the meeting doesn't accomplish much. But no one moves to end it. It is a reassuring "security blanket" for the people who attend, a regular pause in the day's hectic activities.

In some organizations, it is not unusual for managers to call meetings spontaneously, expecting everybody to show up and disregarding other priorities. Or managers may call meetings without announcing the purpose. Or they may convene a meeting when a telephone conversation would suffice. Meetings may be used for show-and-tell, for personal public relations, or for political warfare. Unnecessary or unproductive meetings devour huge amounts of potentially productive time.

Impulsive Actions

Some managers are programmed to move into action whenever they become uneasy about a problem or crisis. Their guiding principle is, "Don't just stand there, do something." They may pick up the phone and give an order to a subordinate. If the problem resurfaces later the manager may assign it to another subordinate.

Whenever the national sales manager for one office equipment supplier got uneasy about results, he launched a new sales contest. In quieter, calmer moments, he would admit that there were too many contests, and that the incentives had no sustained effect on performance. But in the heat of battle, this realization did not stop him from creating yet another contest.

Each time an impulsive manager zigs or zags, others are pulled along in the frantic dance. Several impulsive managers working in the same operation can stimulate a high level of activity but they occasionally cancel each other out. Only rarely do they propel the organization any closer to its goal.

An Infinite Variety of Idiosyncracies

There are as many behavior patterns as there are managers to manifest them. One kind of manager always wants to be present when one of his subordinates is meeting his boss. Some managers never commit themselves in writing. Others are ill at ease in large groups, so they work with their subordinates one at a time. But still other managers are threatened by private meetings with individual subordinates.

Some managers become uneasy when they must listen to others, particularly subordinates; others have trouble accepting criticism of contradictory opinions. Some managers favor frequent travel, and just keep bouncing around from city to city. Others are compulsive talkers. The president of a large metropolitan hospital had his hair cut in his office while conducting meetings because it gave him a sense of total dedication to his job.

Managers' busyness behavior, idiosyncratic patterns, and impulsive actions not only dissipate their own energies, but influence the behavior of others around them. Thus, even minor manifestations of these anxiety-avoidance behaviors can have enormous ramifications as they ripple through an organization influencing the work patterns of dozens or hundreds of other people.

To see how these patterns might be slowing down the organization you selected, fill in Diagnostic Work Sheet 2–2.

DIAGNOSTIC WORK SHEET 2–2

❯❯ *Wasteful Work Patterns and Time Misuse*

Organization _____

Improvement Needed _____

To what extent is progress toward this goal being slowed down by wasteful work patterns or time misuse? Rate each statement according to how accurately it describes the actions of managers responsible for the goal.

	A Great Deal	Somewhat	Not Much (or Not at All)
The managers:			
Follow old, familiar patterns that aren't working	_____	_____	_____
Are "too busy" to focus on critical goals	_____	_____	_____
Impulsively try one thing and then another	_____	_____	_____
Hold inefficient or inappropriate meetings	_____	_____	_____
Overlook or ignore the inputs of others	_____	_____	_____
Engage in other wasteful patterns (Name them)			
_____	_____	_____	_____
_____	_____	_____	_____
_____	_____	_____	_____

❯❯ *Barrier 3: Weak Performance Expectations*

In most organizations, establishment of performance expectations is one of the weakest management skills. Making tough demands increases the risk of unpleasant resistance and challenges by subordinates, which can expose a manager's uncertainties, weaknesses, or lack of knowledge. Subordinates may complain to others. They may quit.

Increased expectations may also elicit the resentment of other managers. If a newly installed manager, for example, asserts that major gains are possible, he implies that his predecessor (or the manager of them both) was content with too little. Even a manager who has been in the job for a while and then goes for major gains raises questions about his earlier performance. And, of course, the higher the goal, the greater the risk of missing it. Setting more modest expectations is an easy out because it reduces all these risks.

Hedged Bets and Escapes

One way to ease the tensions of negotiating goals with subordinates is to permit them some escape hatches. You agree that quality will be improved—provided that suppliers upgrade their materials. Higher output levels will be reached—provided that the new equipment is installed. Sales goals will be achieved—provided that certain new products are released. There is no steadfast commitment to achieve a goal. A signal has been transmitted that no matter what happens, the subordinates can substitute a good explanation for the actual result.

Trades and Backward Delegation

Many managers who are asked for greater performance will negotiate with their boss: they can accomplish the goal, but only if the boss provides fresh support or gets some other group to cooperate. The plant manager explains that if he is to increase output or lower costs, his boss will have to get Labor Relations to clear the way with the union. Thus, as the price of accepting new assignments or higher goals, each subordinate craftily delegates work back to the boss.

Since most managers see themselves as stretched to the limit, they may advise the boss that to accomplish Goal A, they will have to sacrifice Goal B. Some years ago, when Robert Scrivener announced Bell Canada's first, far-reaching cost-improvement program, which launched its transformation, his people took it in stride. "Sure, Bob, we can reduce costs. You just have to tell us where service can be degraded."

Sometimes a subordinate's complaints, feeding into the boss's own sense of guilt, cause the boss to assume major responsibility for the subordinate's tasks. During the introduction of a new product line, one sales manager told his people to call on him if they had trouble with deliveries or needed assistance in selling their customers. Driven by the uneasy feeling that he had asked them to do too much, instead of helping them to solve problems, he jumped in to work the problems out for them.

Hiding in the Bureaucracy

Another way to avoid the discomfort of setting tough performance expectations is to allow the organization's budgeting and goal-setting procedures to act as an impersonal mechanism for performance contracting. The goals from above are passed down with the message, "This is what they've asked for." Or the boss may agree to pass subordinates' goals up the line, saying with a shrug, "I'll submit these, but they may be rejected." Forms are filled out. Reports and computer printouts move from desk to desk. Gradually, the next year's goals and plans evolve from this complex, impersonal process involving many layers of the organization. But accountability has been divided and muddied; individual managers have neither demanded nor received real, personal, individual commitments from their people.

Rewards and Penalties Not Connected to Results

No matter how challenging a goal may be, knowledge that shortfalls can be explained away undermines the seriousness of expectations. A senior manager in one large electronics manufacturer once told me, "What you have to understand about our company is that, if you do a really outstanding job here, you get very well rewarded. And if you do a mediocre job, you also get very well rewarded."

Pronouncements may be made about the importance of reducing costs, improving customer service, or beating out the competition. The fact is, however, in most organizations there is little risk that the failure to achieve major performance goals will have serious personal consequences for managers.

Moreover, no matter how stridently the goals have been announced at the beginning of the year, toward the end of the year people shift attention to setting goals for the next period. Concern with the nearly ended year begins to diminish. "It's too late to do anything about last year. Let's concentrate on setting some really healthy goals for next year."

Finally, many managers have, in addition to their real goals, a long list of goals that must be declared in order to keep senior management pacified. These are usually goals that everyone agrees are important enough to be listed but that do not warrant serious attention. Equal opportunity measures often fall into this category, and there are usually dozens of others. Their appearance on the list year after year undercuts the message that goals must be taken seriously.

Let's revisit the group you've been diagnosing to see how weaknesses in performance demand-making may be limiting performance. See Diagnostic Work Sheet 2–3.

>> Barrier 4: Misuse of Work Management Disciplines

In ancient times "managers" who led great armies or built pyramids had to be on hand to observe events directly and to provide directions to subordinates. The tools of large-scale modern enterprises, however, permit remote influence. Goals can be agreed upon in advance; plans and schedules can spell out how the goals will be reached; measures and reviews permit the tracking of progress against the plan.

These basic work management disciplines are so familiar and so taken for granted that virtually every experienced manager regards them as essential tools in achieving results. And yet, as a consequence of poor habits or avoidance patterns, the misuse of these disciplines often undermines achievement.

Too Many Goals

A manager may set too many goals for himself and his people and may be driven to try covering too many bases. Selecting a few critical goals to concentrate on can involve some difficult

---

DIAGNOSTIC WORK SHEET 2-3

>> *Weak Performance Expectations*

Organization _____

Improvement Needed _____

To what extent is progress toward this goal being slowed down by weaknesses in performance expectations? Rate each statement according to how accurately it describes the actions of managers responsible for the goal.

	A Great Deal	Somewhat	Not Much (or Not at All)
The managers:			
Have asked for too little (modest demands)	_____	_____	_____
Permit subordinates too many escape hatches	_____	_____	_____
Allow subordinates to sacrifice one goal to achieve another	_____	_____	_____
Accept explanations in place of results	_____	_____	_____
Accept backward delegation	_____	_____	_____
Don't assure real consequences for success or failure of subordinates	_____	_____	_____
Weaken expectations in other ways (Name them)			
_____	_____	_____	_____
_____	_____	_____	_____
_____	_____	_____	_____

---

choices. So these managers act like investors who, uncertain which way to go, invest $50 each in dozens of different stocks and bonds. "Our boss," said one vice president, "feels free to pass on every new idea he gets. He never asks whether we have the time or resources to work on them, he just keeps passing them on." Deciding not to pursue certain goals may be too discomforting and so managers may try to pursue them all.

Goals Set Too Far in the Future

The evidence is overwhelming that human enthusiasm and energy is aroused most by goals that can be attained quickly. Nevertheless, few organizations make sufficient effort to organize their annual goals into short-term subgoals. Instead, people are expected to maintain a high effort as they slog toward goals they can only attain months or even years later. For example, a new product development project that requires eighteen months of straight-out, disciplined, nose-to-the-grindstone work may afford team members only a single reinforcing moment of success—and then only if they complete the project on schedule.

Elusive Goals

Often managers set goals that are vague or unmeasurable. The sales vice president of a pharmaceutical company launches a new product with the promise to "take a significant step up in market share." A plant manager announces that "quality must be significantly improved in the next quarter." Everyone present nods their head in agreement. The railroad superintendent declares "Eliminating train accidents is everyone's top goal." These vague goals are meaningless.

Unclear or Incomplete Work Plans

Given the complexity of most management tasks that involve more than one or two people, there is no way to succeed without clear work plans that describe who is going to do what, with whom, and when. This set of agreements needs to be written out so that managers can plan their own tasks and coordinate them with the plans of others.

The marketing vice president of a machine tool company complained that his subordinates weren't achieveing nearly what they had agreed to achieve. In searching for the reasons, I asked whether those goals and expectations had been expressed in writing. "They don't have to be written down," he responded, "they are etched like steel in my mind." The rationalization permitted him to avoid the hard work of clearly defining and communicating expectations.

At a recent meeting, I observed a group of managers attempting to speed the flow of work through a machine shop. Many ideas were discussed and accepted. Production scheduling was going to make some changes. Some of the parts were going to be given to a vendor. The third shift would be expanded. As the meeting went on, each manager took notes on what was to be done. At the end of the meeting the manufacturing manager summarized, "Well, it looks as though we've licked the problem. Do you all agree?" They all did, and off they went, each with his own view of what had to be done. Within a week, it was clear that the results were not going to be achieved. How can you produce a symphony when each player writes his own score? This type of behavior is commonplace: managers agree on actions, but fail to create a unified work plan that spells out each person's part.

Most often, the more complex, exploratory, or uncertain elements in a project are not detailed. This may occur because the managers don't know how to do it, or because their company culture does not require it. Sometimes plans are not created because it is easier or less anxiety-provoking to avoid the discipline of nailing down commitments.

Incomplete Tracking and Review

Managers in a number of organizations have said to me, "We are great starters in this company—but we're not too good at finishing." What they mean is that they define needs, develop plans to achieve them, get started on those plans, and have a review session or two. Then other priorities come along, and the earlier goals are sidelined. Even when they have clearly established goals and work plans, they may not review progress consistently and persistently.

This occurs commonly on long-term projects like new systems development and new product development. When a new product idea is first being crystallized, the designs and specifications are being formulated, and the technical pathways are being plotted, there is tremendous interest and energy. Then, as the long, hard months pass, progress reviews may be slighted or delegated to lower levels. Only as the day approaches when the product is scheduled for manufacture is it suddenly discovered that the project is going to be months late.

Fuzzy Accountability

Another way by which managers unwittingly undermine performance capability is through vagueness or ambiguity in assigning accountability for the achievement of goals.

When senior managers tell me about major projects—such as developing a new product, or introducing a new process, or achieving a major productivity gain—I always ask, "Who is responsible for the result?" They almost always respond by naming a number of individuals, each bearing a piece of the responsibility. Managers maintain their psychological comfort by assuming full responsibility only for getting things done within their own territories. Each does a piece of the job—but responsibility for the ultimate result is always someone else's. This thinking, carried to the ultimate, makes it possible for every manager in a business unit to be rated "outstanding" even when the unit has done poorly.

There is a widely accepted notion that if a manager doesn't have full authority over the resources needed to achieve a goal, he or she should not be held accountable for the goal. This is nothing more than a collective rationalization. The complexity of organizational life makes it impossible for any one manager to have full authority over the resources needed for any but the simplest task. Letting managers escape ultimate responsibility for results makes the company president the ultimate manager of every project.

By these and other devices, basic performance ability falls far short of accomplishing its purpose. These notions of accountability that we all take so much for granted are actually serious handicaps.

On Diagnostic Work Sheet 2–4 expand your diagnosis by considering whether some of these weaknesses in work management disciplines are impeding the work of your selected group.

DIAGNOSTIC WORK SHEET 2-4

›› *Work Management Disciplines*

Organization _____

Improvement Needed _____

To what extent is progress toward this goal being slowed down by misuse of work management disciplines? Rate each statement according to how accurately it describes the actions of managers responsible for the goal.

	A Great Deal	Somewhat	Not Much (or Not at All)
The managers have established:			
Too many goals	_____	_____	_____
Goals too long-term	_____	_____	_____
Vague or unmeasurable goals	_____	_____	_____
Weak or incomplete work plans	_____	_____	_____
Infrequent or ineffective review sessions	_____	_____	_____
Other weaknesses in work management disciplines (Name them)			
_____	_____	_____	_____
_____	_____	_____	_____
_____	_____	_____	_____

›› *Barrier 5: Invisible Conspiracy: The Underside of Corporate Culture*

When groups of managers share common rationalizations and avoidance mechanisms, the resulting patterns of behavior take root in the organization. Gradually, each company's formal systems, organization structure, budgeting procedures, and reward systems begin to reflect those enervating patterns. This unwitting and unconscious conspiracy among managers helps to shape the organization's basic culture as much as the positive, productive elements the same managers consciously introduce to make the organization succeed.

Confused Decisionmaking Process

In some companies, the process for making decisions is murky. Putting oneself on the line is risky, so intricate maneuvers obscure exactly when a decision has been made. For example, an office machine manufacturer was debating whether to downplay its rental program in favor of direct sales and long-term leasing. The decision involved some high risks—but also the possibility of a good payoff. Senior management waffled; no clear-cut steps were agreed upon for arriving at a decision. "Signals" were sent out to the field that leasing and sales should be favored over rentals. As these mysterious messages traveled further from headquarters, they became more distorted. This led to a costly "wait and see" attitude instead of a much needed aggressive approach to the market.

In one consumer electronics company, the sophisticated components are designed by engineers in an orderly and disciplined fashion. But it is a long-standing custom that any senior manager can offer advice on styling, color, position of control buttons, and so forth. While this kind of input slows new product development and often leads to bad decisions, the custom is too firmly embedded to be changed.

Low Performance Norms

The unwitting collusion among managers within an organization can lead to the perpetuation of low standards and expectations. Top management talks bravely of ambitious goals, but each layer of managers factors in more and more safety margins and other modifiers to their commitments to reach those goals. Rationalizations are shared, until everybody agrees that 12 percent before tax earnings represent a tremendous achievement. Then some other company comes along and demonstrates that 18 percent or 20 percent can be earned.

When Robert Scrivener first launched his cost reduction and productivity effort at Bell Canada, the company was using the same measurement system as the AT&T system in the United States. As noted in Chapter 1 the notion was deeply embedded in the Bell Canada culture that the average performance of AT&T companies was an acceptable level of performance at Bell Canada. If you were achieving at "system average" or better, you were safe. You only had to worry if you were performing below that standard. Scrivener realized that this long-established performance norm was going to be one of his biggest obstacles. We'll see in Chapter 12 what it took to break down this norm.

The Habit of Accretion

Most companies have a vast capacity to add on new products, new staff functions, new departments, new facilities, and new procedures and controls. When a new report is needed, it is added to the collection of others. One large corporation had a creative group of senior managers who were always launching new performance improvement and employee relations programs that involved standing committees, division goals, and new activities, reviews, and training. Unfortunately, there were no clear mechanisms for ending the programs. The middle managers were overextended and distracted by an ever-expanding series of demands on their time because, like most companies, this one didn't know how to eliminate activities that were no longer useful.

Change as Crisis, Not Routine

In some organizations, changes such as the introduction of a new product or a new technology or a major reorganization are viewed as intrusions. They are put off as long as possible. Studies are conducted; there is a long windup; and then finally, the change is launched. At this point, all the managers expect serious disruption and insist on having time to stabilize before any further changes are introduced.

How many of these invisible cultural patterns are getting in the way of the group you have been analyzing since the start of this chapter? See Diagnostic Work Sheet 2–5.

DIAGNOSTIC WORK SHEET 2–5

» *Invisible Conspiracy: The Corporate Culture Patterns*

Organization _____

Improvement Needed _____

To what extent is progress toward this goal being slowed down by counterproductive corporate cultural patterns? Rate each statement according to how accurately it describes the actions of managers responsible for the goal.

	A Great Deal	Somewhat	Not Much (or Not at All)
The managers are permitting:			
Confused decision-making processes	_____	_____	_____
Low performance norms	_____	_____	_____
Habits of accretion	_____	_____	_____
Change as crisis, not routine	_____	_____	_____
Other cultural patterns (Name them)			
_____	_____	_____	_____
_____	_____	_____	_____
_____	_____	_____	_____

» *Stifled Performance Improvement and Limited Strategic Innovation*

Every organization is more or less afflicted with these invisible barriers that inhibit performance and gradually become institutionalized in its systems, practices, policies, and customs.

This is not to say that people aren't motivated to do the best possible job. By and large, the overwhelming majority of people we encounter would like to do well. They would like to feel proud of the job they are doing and would like to be working for a successful organization. They are frustrated by what they perceive as organizational inefficiencies and roadblocks beyond their control.

Even in the most successful companies that, with great effort, have created practices and work patterns designed to encourage high performance and creativity, the barriers limit performance. And in the great majority of companies, the barriers have so permeated the culture that they severely impede productive capacity—the basic ability of managers to get the work accomplished.

Thus, vast quantities of energy and effort are wasted. Talent and skill are not tapped. The actual productive output of the company may reflect only a small portion of what's being paid for and is potentially available. And the worst of it is that, because the patterns are so ingrained and invisible, senior managers don't appreciate the power of these forces to limit performance and subvert even the most strenuous efforts to accelerate the pace of change.

3

>> *Perpetual Preparations Waste Billions*

The actions that managers take when performance must be improved are profoundly influenced by the fact that they are largely unaware of the vast resources locked up within their organizations, as well as of the barriers that keep those resources imprisoned. Managers sincerely believe that they are producing about as much as anyone could with the resources they manage. So it is natural that when they want to produce more, they begin with a call for new resources, new methods, or new technology. Managers rarely think about extracting more *out* of what they manage until they have first put more *into* it.

The consequence is that in the attempt to get back into the competitive race, management has launched a burgeoning, bewildering quest for programs and systems that will provide salvation, a quest that guarantees that managers will not look where they should for the answers—to their own leadership and to their own capacity to achieve results. Let's see how it worked in a real situation.

>> *Bonaventure Terminal: Target for Improvement*

Located near the downtown core in Montreal, the Bonaventure Express Terminal of the Canadian National Railway was part of a nationwide express network. The huge building had several miles of tracks and platforms running through it. Each day, about 50,000 rail shipments from hundreds of cities and towns were loaded and unloaded. Trucks lined up outside the building, delivering goods to be shipped elsewhere and receiving loads to be delivered locally.

Service quality had declined steadily over the years. For example, overnight service between Montreal and Toronto was promised—but happened only about 45 percent of the time. Costs were out of line. Overtime was a daily occurrence. This terminal is noteworthy, however, not for its poor performance at that time but for the fact that it was one of the most "improved upon" businesses in existence.

Over the years, half a dozen consulting firms had studied the terminal; some focused on layout, while others zeroed in on the handling of materials, or on new ways of scheduling the work flow through the terminal. Management adopted the recommendations they were able to carry out.

During the same period, a team of company industrial engineers was assigned permanently to the terminal. They performed work sampling studies and circulated the perpetually dismal results. They compiled analyses to determine how crews should be scheduled and supervised. And they devised productivity and performance measurements.

The company's human-resource groups were also contributing. Supervisors were trained. Employee attitudes were surveyed, and meetings were held to improve those attitudes. Several experimental projects were designed to involve employees in problem-solving and to make their jobs more interesting. Because the terminal's managers alleged that its poor performance was due to late trains, not to their own shortcomings, "conflict resolution" sessions were held with managers from the department that ran the trains.

Over time, the terminal managers became somewhat fatigued by the unending parade of improvement programs, but they generally cooperated and did what they could to make the programs work. Nevertheless, the bottom-line effects of all the efforts were indiscernible. In fact, performance actually deteriorated slightly during the several years in which all these improvement efforts were being tried.

All of the improvement programs at Bonaventure were introduced by qualified professionals. All were competently carried out. Yet none of them broke through the entrenched work patterns and resistance to change that enveloped the terminal like a dense fog. None of the programs forced Bonaventure's managers to see that they could improve service significantly even if the trains failed to run regularly. Nor did the programs instill a "must-do" attitude about improving performance. Thus, while some of the new techniques and practices produced temporary gains, they all faded as managers and employees drifted back into familiar ways of working.

» *Gearing Up, Gearing Up*

Bonaventure's experience reflects in microcosm the great disappointments that many managers have experienced after investing time, money, and energy in major improvement programs. It demonstrates how the embedded, insidious barriers can prevent even the most professionally installed programs and technologies from producing significant bottom-line results.

Since managers lack a good alternative, when one program fails to produce the desired results, the next one is wheeled into place. When modest efforts don't achieve the gains, more ambitious ones are tried. Managers whose organizations fail to benefit as promised from the systems, programs, and technologies already in place respond by throwing good money after bad.

This is not an anti-intellectual treatise. Some of the tools and techniques that will be discussed are extremely valuable. What I am challenging is the widespread assumption that simply installing enough new programs and new technologies will lead to greater performance in the absence of significant strengthening of the company's capacity to exploit these innovations. Let's look at what happens when these attempts are made.

Automation and Other Manufacturing Innovations

As American industries saw themselves outpaced by overseas competitors, many who could afford it made heavy investments in automation and other forms of computer-assisted design and manufacture. Achieving success in a major manufacturing innovation such as automation, however, means that employees must learn to work differently and supervisors must supervise differently. Maintenance processes are new and different. Parts, machinery, and assembly methods must be designed for the automated process. Design groups must change their procedures. For new product design to be successful, marketing groups must participate in the changes.

It should be evident that successful automation requires fundamental restructuring of most jobs, working relationships, and processes—not just in the directly affected areas but well beyond them. Too many managers, however, fail to deal with these fundamental performance issues and, instead, put their faith and trust—and investment—in the technology itself.

In the past ten years, for example, American automobile manufacturers have invested more than $40 billion in automated manufacturing. The results? According to the June 16, 1987 issue of *Business Week*, "Although Detroit's newest plants are at least as sophisticated as anything in Japan, the productivity at many of what were supposed to be the fanciest production showcases in the U.S. is way short of expectations."

The *Wall Street Journal* of May 13, 1986 reports that the General Motors plant in Hamtramck, Michigan, "has 260 robots for welding, assembly and painting cars, 50 automated guided vehicles to ferry parts to the assembly lines, and a battery of cameras and computers that use laser beams to inspect and control the manufacturing process." Many months after going into production, however, Hamtramck "is turning out only 30 to 35 cars an hour, far less than the 60 an hour it was designed to build." GM is not alone. Referring to the Aerostar mini-van operation in St. Louis, the *Wall Street Journal* also reported that "Ford had to struggle to get computer-controlled machinery from two dozen different suppliers to communicate. Then the company realized that its equipment was so sophisticated that workers could not properly operate it, even after months of training."

An article on robotics in the August 16, 1987 *New York Times* conveys the messianic zeal typical of the purveyors of technological salvation:

Just a few years ago, many top industrialists were capti-
vated by the idea that robots and other computer-based
machines could provide American companies with a deci-
sive competitive edge. The slogan of the times, coined
by the General Electric Company, became "Automate,
Emigrate or Evaporate." Hundreds of millions of dollars
worth of robots were sold during the early part of the
decade.

The article also conveys the bitter disappointments that arise
when the technological fixes don't bring the hoped for salvation:

The sales wars generated losses for most suppliers and
stories of robots that failed to perform as expected . . .
"You couldn't count on them," said Jeffrey Gage, a former
salesman and sales executive for Unimation, Sweden's
ASEA and Advanced Robotics. . . . But there also were
problems when robots performed as specified. True mod-
ernization turned out to require sweeping reforms in the
organization of work, product design and the way inventory was managed . . . Robots could create costly bottle-
necks when misapplied or used to manufacture products
that had not been designed for automated assembly.

The moral of these stories is that even the best innovation
money can buy will not produce the desired results if the ability
to make good use of the innovation does not also expand. Failure
to understand this simple thesis, or the inability to act effectively on it, has led to the waste of untold sums of money and
of management time and energy.

Employee Involvement and Quality Circles

For many years, the human relations movement stressed the fact
that employees have unique perspectives on what is going on
in their parts of the organization. If management were able to
tap into these perspectives, they would be able to obtain useful
ideas on improving operations. Beyond that, showing management's interest in employee views would boost morale.

Most American industry did not do much with these insights until it was observed that successful Japanese companies
involved their people in problem solving and in elaborate employee suggestion systems. Hopeful of replicating Japanese

results, many companies then sought ways to tap into employee ideas. But instead of treating employee involvement as one strand of a comprehensive fabric of change, companies typically expected employee involvement itself to provide the "open sesame" to quality and productivity.

During the 1970s and early 1980s, these expectations were reinforced by the "quality circle" movement which provided neat packages of formal training, special vocabulary, and associations of practitioners.

The experience of one small plant in South Carolina, which manufactures rubber timing belts for the automobile industry, illustrates what happens all too often. Keeping quality standards high in the precision machining of rubber is extremely difficult, and this plant was not doing very well. Because of frequent and costly reworking they often missed promised shipping dates—an unforgivable sin in the automotive industry. Their human-resource group convinced plant management that they should enlist their employees to help solve the problem, and a quality circle program was launched. Employees and supervisors were trained in "problem-solving techniques," and a schedule of committee meetings was set up. Employees were invited to participate on a voluntary basis.

The employee teams had their meetings. They identified problems and made many recommendations for improving working conditions and operations. Supervisors and plant engineers, who already felt stretched, added the quality circle recommendations to their long lists of "action items," and they tried to implement them when they could find the time and resources to do so. The weekly quality circle meetings did not, however, change the basic way supervisors viewed their jobs or how they worked with their people on a day-to-day basis. The program did not place any additional expectations for achievement on the supervisors. In fact, they felt somewhat relieved of responsibility, as everyone looked to the quality circles to somehow produce quality improvement. Everyone liked the activity. The only hitch was that quality was not materially improved.

This pattern has been repeated in countless companies. The word goes out that employee involvement is "in," and units gear up to respond. Staff groups and outside consultants spring into action to create training programs, manuals, and communications procedures. Millions of dollars are spent. But when the programs are not accompanied by stronger demands for results, or by help to managers to produce those results, lackluster performance persists and expectations are dashed.

Company Reorganizations

The president of a large electronics manufacturer had been under pressure from his board of directors for almost a year to improve results and to accelerate the company's entry into several new markets. He attributed the lack of progress to the organization's structure. "We're just not organized right to make this happen. With our functional structure, there's no real commitment to 'winning' in any specific marketplace. We need to organize in terms of how we want to face our customers."

With board approval, the president called in a consulting firm. They took a number of months to do a thorough organization study and to develop recommendations. It took many more months for those recommendations to be analyzed, digested, and acted upon. The president was very active in the study, and it actually gave him a whole new outlook on his predicament. Before the study, he would become very defensive when pressed to explain poor results. Gradually, he became more confident and assertive. "That's right," he would agree, when shortcomings were pointed out. "Just more proof that we're structured all wrong." He also used the study to defer decisions "until we know which way we're heading."

Finally, after two years of studies and preparations, the new organization structure was in place. During this time, few of the other changes essential to success were being introduced. Ultimately, the reorganization contributed nothing to rejuvenating the company's performance.

Reorganizations often tempt frustrated managers. One bold stroke, after all, might enable the company or division to overcome barriers and problems. Some companies eliminate whole layers of management, while others break units into smaller profit centers. But no matter how the structure may change, until a company's basic capacity to perform improves, the outcome is likely to be no more than one would expect from the same old components just rearranged into a new configuration.

Information Systems and Computer Technology

Because computer-based information systems have become so vital, it is natural to depend on those systems as a critical success ingredient. Companies invest larger and larger sums on their information systems, with an almost mystical faith in what the technology will do.

A manufacturer of electronic office equipment was seeing its business expand rapidly over a broad geographic area. The company established a strong corporate systems group with a virtually unlimited budget to create systems necessary to serve their rapidly expanding clientele. The corporate vice president for MIS proudly described their materials management system as "one of the most sophisticated available in the world today."

At that very moment, however, at a plant a thousand miles from headquarters, foremen and workers were scurrying around trying to assemble kits to meet overdue orders. Bills of materials and other documentation were defective. There were parts shortages and delays, and huge amounts of overtime were needed to get the job done.

Yes, the technical system was sophisticated all right, but all of the other organization activities and subsystems that had to mesh with it were less so. Like a $75,000 automobile with a flat tire, the system was no more powerful than the organization's ability to make it work.

Training and Management Development

Another favorite panacea for business ills is training and management development programs. If we expect people to do something better or different, we have to train them first. Correct? Of course! And so thousands and thousands of managers, supervisors, engineers, and employees are deployed for training.

Where those training programs teach specific, technical job skills and procedures, there may be real payoffs. But where the training is aimed at general management techniques, leadership styles, entrepreneurial skills, and the like, there is rarely a measurable connection between the training and subsequent performance improvement. Senior managers who smile with amusement at the baseball player who ritualistically touches his cap and his numbers and taps his bat on the ground before stepping up to the plate, routinely allocate hundreds of thousands of dollars to training activities whose link to the desired results may be just as wishful as the ball player's superstitions.

Several years ago, I met a senior staff person for a large airline while traveling on that airline. I asked how things were going—knowing that the company was encountering considerable difficulty and was losing money. "Great," he responded enthusiastically, to my surprise. I inquired further, to discover what was so "great," and he said, "We have put over 400 managers through our 'management by objectives' program this year—and another 200 are scheduled to participate." He went on to describe in glowing terms how top management was "100 percent behind the effort."

He and his top management seemed to be ignoring all the built-in impediments to competitive performance that handicapped that organization: vice presidents of marketing, planning, and operations who had conflicting views on policy; a management that had never been required to improve performance; and employees who spent more energy on their "rights" than on their achievements. There was no way that management training would overcome those barriers and lead to real performance changes. But for more than a year, the costly training effort permitted management to believe they were really attacking the airline's competitive challenges.

Financial Incentives

Another step along the search for the holy grail of competitive success is the use of "incentives," which usually take the form of additional financial rewards. Based on the implicit beliefs that (a) more individual motivation is the key to greater effectiveness and that (b) this performance-producing motivation can be sustained by the promise of future goodies, people are told that if they can improve performance by X percent they will earn Y dollars. It is important, of course, to share corporate gains with those who help create them. But there is little evidence to suggest that corporate performance gains can be sustained by dangling morsels of reward—as though teaching a dog to sit.

One recently deregulated public utility, for example, installed an incentive pay package to speed progress toward making its services more competitive with "lean and mean" competitors. Instead of facing up to the very difficult job of raising performance standards, management took the shortcut of waving rewards around. Now the company is saddled with a costly, time-consuming incentive program—and *still* has ahead of it the enormous task of achieving high performance and becoming more entrepreneurial and competitive.

"Theme" Programs and Corporate Extravaganzas

Another common approach to improving performance is to engage the entire organization in a process centered around a theme—Total Quality, Culture Change, Service Excellence. Huge investments are made in these programs, and support for them becomes a test of loyalty for managers.

One very large company was so enamored with theme programs that they needed a special chart to describe the relationships among over forty different ones they had going. Nowhere on the chart was there a reference to bottom-line results. It was assumed that with all that good activity, results would swiftly follow. When the evidence failed to support the assumption, the "solution" was to devote even more energy to the activities.

❱❱ *Stalled in the Starting Gate*

While the programs and technologies described in this chapter can contribute to major performance improvements, too often they are introduced in ways that fail to yield significant results. When that happens, management may then discard the program, concluding that they adopted the wrong one. Meanwhile, they've heard about a powerful program that really helped some other company, and so they take a deep breath and leap onto the new bandwagon.

If managers are to develop more effective means for improving performance, they must understand the reasons why all of these programs have so often failed to produce the expected gains.

First, most of these improvement efforts are too narrow; they are designed to influence only a few specific corporate activities. This is true even of the large-scale corporate extravaganzas, to say nothing of more focused industrial engineering studies, training programs, automation, or restructuring.

Frequently, these improvement efforts are launched by managers who lack skill in establishing higher performance expectations. They place their faith in the programs to produce the results and thus avoid having to examine and change how they work with their people.

Further, the programs often fail to convey a sense of "ownership" by the people who will use them. Most productivity, quality, and other improvement programs are the products of the staff organizations and consulting firms who are introducing them. Managers carry on with their regular jobs while the experts wheel the programs into place. When innovative tools, methods, and approaches are placed in the hands of people who aren't enthusiastic about using them or don't have any strong motivation to improve, no one should be surprised if the results are meager.

And finally, instead of focusing directly on achieving a measurable end result (like lower costs, better quality, faster turnaround time), many improvement programs never get beyond the preparatory stage. The assumption is that once there has been enough gearing up, enough training, enough investment, results will someday emerge like Venus from the sea. And because they rarely require managers to get more yield at once from their current people, resources, and systems, these programs actually reinforce managers' rationalizations that they are doing about as well as possible with what they have.

In *Through the Looking Glass*, the White Queen tells Alice: "The rule is 'Jam yesterday and jam tomorrow but never jam today'" That could be the motto for many corporations today. We look back on the past, when our companies were invincible. When will we prevail once again? Very soon—just wait. Wait until we have introduced our new management information system. Wait until the new products being designed replace the old ones. Wait until all 20,000 employees have been put through quality training programs. Wait until we have the new production planning and control system. Wait until we reorganize. Wait until we break big units up into small profit centers. Wait, wait, wait. Spend, spend, spend. Meanwhile, jam yesterday and jam tomorrow.

The Silver Lining

The frustration and shortfalls that result from overreliance on programs and preparations are exacting a horrible toll on American industry. The bad news is that huge investments are being made that are not paying off. Valuable management energy, expense, and capital investments are being poured into the effort while time slips away!

But, the good news is that there is something every company can do about it. Starting at once. The key is to focus first not on installing programs but on upgrading management's performance capacity and its ability to benefit from innovation. How? In Chapter 1, we saw that emergencies and crises often spontaneously generate huge rises in output and effectiveness, without any significant changes having been made. All managers have seen this phenomenon—but most dismiss it as having no fundamental importance. Let's now take a closer look at crisis dynamics.

PART II

The Breakthrough Strategy: Success as the Building Block

4

>> *The Zest Factors Reveal What's Possible*

Business emergencies, crises, and natural disasters suddenly liberate organizations from the restraints of the institutionalized barriers to performance improvement. These events evoke powerful and dramatic responses that cannot be matched by any of the structured programs and technologies described in the previous chapter. Consider these experiences.

When adulterated Tylenol capsules caused the deaths of seven people in September 1982, Johnson & Johnson organized a crash program to protect the public as well as to salvage its successful product. One of the most critical tasks was to design a sealed package. Within about seven weeks, a team of engineers and designers had developed and tested a triple-sealed package, redesigned production processes and equipment, developed new package graphics, and moved into full-scale production. Completing this series of complex tasks under normal circumstances would have taken well over a year.

On February 27, 1975, a five-alarm fire completely gutted the Second Avenue switching station of the New York Telephone Company, an eleven-story building filled with complex equipment. Telephone service to the southern end of Manhattan, including the whole financial district and the police and fire departments, was cut off. Within hours, work teams had rolled in mobile equipment trailers and connected them to provide emergency service. Within days, most of the service was restored. In less than three weeks, telephone service was back to normal. It was called the "miracle on Second Avenue."

When I was giving a seminar in Caracas some years ago, the officer responsible for information systems on the largest construction project ever undertaken in Venezuela, the building of the Caracas subway, recounted the following story. One morning he was informed that the president of Venezuela would be visiting the project the next day. This would require gathering and analyzing information that ordinarily took about two weeks to develop, within twenty-four hours. He described how he and his people got organized so that they actually delivered the data on time—in fact, ahead of the deadline. What shocked him was the fact that the reports, which on the two-week cycle usually required days of "cleaning up," were relatively error-free. Not only the amount but the quality of work done was dramatically upgraded in this crisis.

❯❯ *Too Good to Be Real?*

Every time I ask a group of managers about their own crisis-provoked "miracles," there is no end to the stories they recount. Virtually every manager has seen it happen. But when the crisis passes, they almost always overlook the profound significance of what the crisis revealed.

They see their people rise to great heights of performance—and then accept it when those same people sink back to "normal." They even seem threatened when it is suggested that their unit can sustain the higher performance. No, they respond, our unit can't possibly do that—except by burning out our people, or by focusing on one task at the expense of others, or by keeping the organization stirred up in perpetual crises. And with these rationalizations, managers turn away from what is potentially one of the most valuable learning opportunities in their experience.

If we consider that the heightened performance we see in emergencies and crises usually occurs almost spontaneously, without the benefit of extensive management planning, we can only imagine the possibilities for greater performance if the galvanizing forces of the crises were to be combined with purposeful management action. It is clear that what managers regard as "normal" levels of operation are generally only a fraction of what the organization is really capable of achieving.

Of course, I won't recommend that companies run in crisis mode, burn out their people with sixteen-hour days, do one thing well and drop the rest. But if we examine these events, we'll see graphically what it is that allows organizations to break through their built-in barriers and perform at high levels. These lessons can be applied in an orderly way to the ongoing management of the organization.

I have asked thousands of managers to identify what they believe to be the critical forces eliciting extraordinary performance in such crises. No matter where in the Western world, no matter what kind of managers, and no matter what their level of sophistication, they cite essentially the same list of reasons for these spurts in performance.

Before looking at what everyone else thinks, you might like to get into the act. Think of a situation that you have witnessed or heard about in which some emergency or crisis caused a group to perform at levels very far above normal. Before looking ahead, ask yourself: *What were the key factors in the situation that elicited the unusually high performance?* What caused the group to perform at levels that were way beyond normal? Think of at least four or five factors, if you can, and write them down. Now compare your factors to the list of "zest factors" on the next page.

Zest Infuses a Motorola Project

It is not only crises that mobilize the zest factors. Sometimes exceptionally challenging business goals knock down the old barriers and inspire people to exceptional performance.

❯❯ *The Zest Factors*

Why do crises stimulate radically higher performance?

❯ Sense of urgency
❯ A challenge
❯ Success near and clear
❯ People collaborate—a new "esprit"
❯ Pride of achievement
❯ Fear of failure
❯ Exciting, novel, like a game
❯ People experiment and ignore "red tape"

Motorola, for a number of years, has had a strategy for competing in Japan. The chairman, Bob Galvin, and his top-management colleagues became convinced that only by competing directly in the home marketplace of the best Japanese companies could Motorola learn how to compete on equal or better terms anywhere else.

Several years ago, Motorola's Communications Sector had a chance to become a supplier to Nippon Telephone and Telegraph for a certain kind of pager—the small radio device that permits signals or messages to be transmitted to individuals wherever they might be. The up side was that Motorola was one of the very few companies outside of Japan respected enough to be asked for a bid on this business. The down side was that the time allowed for developing the product was less than two-thirds of what Motorola considered a reasonable new product development cycle. Moreover, the quality standards were so far beyond what had been viewed as reasonable (even by Motorola, which had been driving for constant improvement in its own standards) that many Motorola managers considered them virtually "impossible." The shortness of time precluded any search for new technology to accomplish the results. Success would depend solely on the way people worked together to get the job done. A team was assembled, and the importance of the goal emphasized to all.

Any innovations that could help to achieve the results on a sustainable basis were encouraged from the beginning. For example, the group took the radical step of agreeing that the acceptable level of defects was to be zero—absolutely zero. Any defect at all was to be considered unacceptable, and whatever produced it was to be investigated. In electronics manufacture, it is customary to touch up minor defects by soldering on additional components or by replacing faulty components. This was ruled out—no repairs would be permitted on any product to be shipped.

Many other innovations were introduced as the teams of managers, engineers, and employees worked together to get the job done. After they succeeded—and they surely did succeed—team members were interviewed to discover what they viewed as the keys to their success. Their words convey the essence of what happened:

> "The customer came and told us that nothing except absolute excellence would be accepted. It was generally considered a suicide mission. The team was really turned on by the challenge of doing something that was considered impossible to do."

> "People were challenged every day. Engineers were working up to 100-hour weeks. They were getting calls at 3:00 in the morning. There was a strong drive to succeed in this program. It was the most exciting time of my life."

> "I remember one night when the group leaders and the engineers were right down in the packing department with the employees, helping them pack boxes. The main thing was to get the job done on time."

> "Everybody shared responsibility. It was clear that if you needed something, or if you saw a problem, it was your job to ask. My boss would not accept any excuse for not asking for what you needed."

> "Perfect work was required—and the schedule required immense personal sacrifice. The team loved it. When each radio started down the line, a small, green-colored sticker was put on the chassis. That sticker remained unless a defect of any kind was discovered during the process. The first time the one-hundredth consecutive radio reached the end with its green sticker still on, the production line stopped and everyone cheered."

Compare these quotations with the zest factors list and notice how many of the factors are reflected in what these people remember so vividly.

Zest Factors Breathe Life into Work

People from other companies who have participated in challenging events and projects similar to the Motorola pager project, or who have found themselves responding to crises or emergencies with unprecedented levels of performance, all say similar kinds of things.

A telecommunications manufacturing executive, about a telephone switch needed to support a major network cutover: "We knew we would lose all the rest of the order if we didn't deliver this one by the end of January. Nobody even raised a question of whether we *could* do it. It was just assumed that we *would* do it."

A foreman, about efforts to keep an electric generating plant on stream during the worst snowstorm in fifty years: "At the height of it you couldn't tell the superintendent from the foreman from the craftsman. They were all fighting the storm together."

The manager of a plant where a critical piece of equipment had been damaged and would be out of service for two months: "It was amazing how fast new ideas came out—and how quickly people were willing to try them. Those ideas must have been kicking around for a long time—but we had the attitude here, as long as it was working okay, why mess with it."

» Extraordinary Versus Normal

The first lesson to be learned from these crises, and from the zest factors they release, is in seeing with new perspective how *unzestful* the daily life in most organizations actually is.

Try it yourself. Think of a major goal that your company or your work group (or some other group you are familiar with) is currently trying to achieve—perhaps the project you had in mind when you were diagnosing corporate barriers in Chapter 2.

Rate this goal on Diagnostic Work Sheet 4–1 according to how much zest is built into it. You will probably make two discoveries:

1. Most of the work that goes on in organizations has depressingly little zest in it. Even when rating a company's most important projects, we find that managers often assign them a "1" or "2" on most of the factors.
2. The exceptions are those few projects—like the Motorola pager—that seem to "catch fire." Ratings on those projects are "4" or "5." High zest and success go hand in hand.

Checking for Zest

Carry out another assessment of the zest levels in your own organization. Over the course of a week, take copies of the zest assessment work sheet with you and rate the zest levels on a sampling of important projects you're involved in. Ask some other managers to try it too, and compare your answers.

Imagine asking a random sampling of managers and employees as they leave work on Friday afternoon: "What did you accomplish this week?" Most managers tell me that the answers they would hear are: "Thank God, it's Friday," and, "Got through the week," and, "Just more of the same old routine." Few people will describe specific accomplishments of which they can be proud. Few had the satisfaction of achieving a meaningful goal. Few have had exciting moments. These reactions do not confirm that zest factors can only be released in crises. What these listless reactions reveal is that most companies utterly fail to create zestful environments.

›› *Go for Results—Now!*

The Breakthrough strategy employs a startlingly simple logic that absolutely reverses the typical view of corporate cause and effect. Stop focusing all your attention on infusing your organization with the right programs, preparations, and technology, in

DIAGNOSTIC WORK SHEET 4-1

>> *Zest Levels*

Rate each factor from 1 (Low) to 5 (High)

Project or Goal _____

1 Low Zest	2	3	4	5 High Zest
The goal is important but there's no real sense of *urgency*				There's a real sense of *urgency*. The goal *must* be achieved.
We don't feel challenged.				We all feel a great sense of challenge.
This is an ongoing effort with no clear "win" point.				Success is clear and measurable.
We're just working in the same old way.				We're really working together to achieve results.
It won't significantly affect us whether we succeed or not.				The stakes are big. We'll be up if we win (and down if we don't).
What a humdrum task.				What an exciting job!
Nobody is willing to stick his neck out.				We're not afraid of mistakes; we'll try anything that might work.

the hope that someday these magic ingredients will make your company a ferocious competitor. Instead, go for a better result at once, now, immediately—exploiting the zest factors to make it happen.

The breakthrough strategy reveals that no matter how busy people look, no matter how desperate the apparent need for more resources or for better information or for more cooperation from others, no matter how weak the systems or how untrained the people, you can achieve better results *right now* with what you already have.

By "results," I mean a measurable success. Reduce inventory by 10 percent (rather than introduce a new inventory system); improve yields by 20 percent (rather than study causes of quality defects); reduce the time it takes to get an important new product to market (rather than redesign the new product development process).

The breakthrough strategy attempts to recreate the zest factors—which release so much force and energy in reaching important short-term goals—and to use them as the wedge to break through institutionalized barriers. Immediate successes are essential if people are to increase their confidence and expand their vision of what is possible.

Stop waiting for a crisis or emergency to show you, for a fleeting moment, what you are really capable of achieving. Through the successful accomplishment of a tangible goal, you can learn to function in new and better ways. You can start getting out from under the weight of day-to-day performance shortcomings and acquire the skills needed to expand your first breakthrough success into a widening circle of greater and greater success.

5

>> Design Each Project for Certain Success

In any organization, at any moment in time, given any shortcomings of people, systems, relationships, methods, or equipment, there is always *something* that can be done right away to improve performance. By focusing on and achieving a specific result, managers can take the first step toward improved competitive performance. This first step is the "breakthrough project"—an organized effort to exploit the zest factors in the achievement of a tangible short-term goal so that managers can experience a reinforcing and confidence-building success.

>> What Is a Breakthrough Project?

A **Planned** Project that uses the Zest Factors to achieve a tangible, bottom-line **result** in **a short period of time**—and that is carried out in ways that generate the new management confidence and new management skills essential for further progress.

Isn't this what most good managers generally do? No. Consider the Bonaventure Terminal case described in Chapter 3: to improve service reliability, many different improvement programs were instituted. Better results were supposed to follow later, as the outcome of these programs. When the better result itself is the starting point, rather than a hoped for consequence, the shift in performance can be dramatic.

When I met with the managers of that terminal, they looked at me with resignation on their faces; here was yet another expert to tell them how to improve service. Instead, I asked them to ignore for the moment all the problems to be overcome and all the improvement programs they had endured. I asked: Was there any improvement, however modest, that they might be able to achieve in a relatively short time if they all put their minds to it? At first they protested that they were doing all they could do. The way to improve service, they advised, was for me to go help the transportation department to get the trains running on time. But after persistent probing, they began to suggest some possible initiatives they could take. They all agreed that they should focus on one key train, No. 242. Recently they had been loading only 45 to 50 percent of the shipments that were supposed to be on that train for overnight delivery to Toronto. They were embarrassed by that performance, they admitted, and after further discussion, they decided to try to increase that figure to 80 percent in the next few months, without affecting service on any other trains.

The focus on a specific, measurable, short-term goal, of their own choosing, which they might achieve without outside cooperation, permission, or expertise, changed the entire psychology of the situation. As they began to work on meeting the challenge, they assumed a personal responsibility for the result. This project gave them some fun and excitement, which had been missing from their jobs. Once they accomplished a significant step toward the goal—which they did in a few weeks—they were no longer the passive losers whom everybody was trying to improve. They were managers who had achieved an important success and were ready to move on to the next challenge.

)) *The Breakthrough Goal*

As in the Bonaventure example, the first, and often the most psychologically difficult, shift is that managers must, for a time at least, put aside their studies, explanations, preparations, preliminaries, training, gearing up, analyses, and programs—and focus on accomplishing a short-term result, a success. The vehicle for doing this is the breakthrough project, which must be "loaded for success" by exploiting the zest factors. Five guidelines for selecting such a goal will help to assure success virtually every time.

1. Begin with an *urgent and compelling* goal. The focus should be on improvements that everybody will clearly and instantly recognize as vital, and necessary *now*, and that are therefore capable of arousing some zest.
2. It is important that people be able to anticipate a first success in a matter of weeks, not months or years. So a *short-term, first-step* subgoal should be extracted from the large, complex, urgent goal.
3. The subgoal should be discrete and focused on a *measurable, bottom-line* result. "Improving inventory turnover" or "reducing inventory," by some measurable amount, are examples of such goals; the more general, "improving inventory procedures," is not a good subgoal.
4. To assure and engage everyone's commitment, the project should exploit what people are *ready, willing, and able* to do—that is, it should not be based on the hope of convincing them of what they *ought* to do.
5. The goal should be achievable with *available resources and authority*—so that those who are carrying out the project can commit themselves, without hedged bets and escape clauses, to producing success.

By selecting a goal that is clearly urgent and setting a first step that can be accomplished in a short time, some of the energizing forces of a crisis can be stimulated in a disciplined, controlled fashion. The Pennwalt Corporation has used the breakthrough strategy in a number of installations. Let's see how one of its chemical processing plants exploited the approach.

» *Breakthrough Project Selection Guidelines*

To assure success, select a goal that:

1. Is **urgent and compelling**—a real attention-getter.
2. Is a **first-step goal** achievable in a short period of time—in weeks rather than months.
3. Is a **bottom-line result**, discrete and measurable.
4. The responsible participants feel **ready, willing,** and **able** to accomplish.
5. Can be achieved with **available resources and authority**.

» *A Pennwalt Plant at the Brink*

In January 1986, Pennwalt Corporation's headquarters informed Wayne O'Quin, manager of its Calvert City, Kentucky plant, that a corporate study to evaluate the plant's future had been initiated. The cost of the plant's key Isotron products—refrigerants used in automobile air conditioners—was too high, and its market position was seriously eroding. After thirty-seven years of operation, the future of the plant and the jobs of its 400 employees were on the line.

No Way Out but Up

Well before this critical point, O'Quin had organized some work teams to study ways to improve operations, but these groups had not as yet produced significant gains. Aware that other Pennwalt managers benefited from using the breakthrough strategy, O'Quinn decided to apply it in getting some fast results from his teams.

He met with the teams, and with the assistance of consultants who had worked with the other plants, described the approach. It was hard to imagine a goal more "urgent and compelling" (Guideline 1) than keeping the plant in business. O'Quin told his people, "Remember, we are on trial. We can't expect approval for any new investment. We have to focus on what we can do better with what we already have" (Guideline 5).

They decided that reducing the cost of hydrofluoric acid, the key feed stock in their Isotron products, was the first priority. Hydrofluoric acid was formed by feeding the mineral fluorspar into a heated kiln with sulfuric acid. In this fiercely competitive business, the costs for hydrofluoric acid at Calvert City were running well above industry standards.

One manager expressed the skepticism they all shared: "We've had eighteen task forces working on hydrofluoric acid production for months, and they haven't made a dent. What are we supposed to do?" That was O'Quin's cue. "That's exactly the problem!" he said. "We've got all these groups looking at too many different aspects of production. Why don't we set a short-term goal for hydrofluoric acid cost reduction and choose just a few projects that could really have some impact."

Cliff Adams, manager of Operations, was given overall responsibility for organizing the effort. To become competitive, he had to reduce the costs of their hydrofluoric acid by at least 18 percent—a huge gain—and do it quickly. Adams worked with the managers of Engineering and Technology to select a few key projects from among the great many already under way. They reviewed progress with all the task force leaders; they went over production cost data; and they estimated the potential savings from each project.

Of all the projects, the one with the biggest potential was the effort to increase the feed rate of raw materials into the kilns. Raising by 20 percent the rate at which raw materials were fed would accomplish half the overall required savings. Cliff Adams thought it could be done and decided to put the main effort here (Guideline 2: a first-step subgoal). The managers who ran the kilns were hesitant to take on the goal. They had tried it a few years back, but the equipment had malfunctioned and they had been forced to slow the feed rate back down. Adams acknowledged their concern by emphasizing that *any* increase in feed rate would have a significant impact on cost, and that they should try to select a goal as close to the 20 percent target as they felt they could possibly meet. (Guideline 4: based on existing readiness).

Moving into Action

When the feed rate–increase team met, with representatives from Operations, Maintenance, Engineering, and Technology, skepticism was the dominant theme. Sonny Rommelman, the subproject leader, urged them not to "get caught up in what we can't control." He asked the group to identify some ideas for steps they *could* take. Slowly the ideas started to come out:

> "Let's make an appointment with the equipment manufacturer to determine exactly what happens metallurgically to the kilns when they are operated at the higher temperatures."

> "We'll have to reschedule our preventive maintenance at the higher feed rates. We didn't do that last time."

> "We have to make some modifications to the instrumentation so it can handle the increased flow rate."

> "We better identify any safety problems and make sure we deal with them."

Rommleman, standing at the front of the room with a newsprint flip chart and magic marker, noted all the suggestions as they emerged. "Keep putting out your ideas," he said. By the time all the initial ideas had been shared, sheets of newsprint covered most of the meeting room's front wall.

The team then reviewed all the suggestions and narrowed them down to the ones they thought were the most feasible and could be accomplished in the near term. "Now comes the hard part," said Rommelman. "For each of these tasks, we have to assign one person to make sure it gets done, and then we have to get a commitment for a completion date." When this was done, the team had made a first cut at a plan for reaching their goal. Although the plan was to be modified later as more ideas arose and some steps proved to be unworkable, when they left the room at the end of that first meeting, everyone knew exactly where to begin.

The previous attempt to operate at higher feed rates had included all six kilns. This time the team started with only one kiln, to learn about the effect of temperature increase, to recalibrate the instruments, and to make a variety of small improvements.

(Here's Guideline 2 again—an even smaller, first-step subgoal—and Guideline 3: aim for measurable, bottom-line results.)

The team slowly began to jack up the feed rate on the one selected kiln. After only two months, they achieved the 20 percent increase, with all operating and maintenance factors under control. All the elements of careful preparation had come together to make it happen. The narrowing-down process and the focus on a very sharply defined goal helped to concentrate everyone's efforts. The short time frame provided an extra sense of urgency. The day-by-day measure of progress provided the drama. And the sweet pleasure of success provided a psychic reward that had been virtually nonexistent in that chronically high-cost operation. In the following weeks, they moved on to the five other kilns, all of which were soon operating at the higher rate. Production costs declined significantly.

The feed rate project success provided the impetus for the other breakthrough projects. Over the course of several months, a series of projects resulted in an overall reduction in hydrofluoric acid manufacturing costs even greater than the necessary 18 percent—with no new investment. With this new cost structure, the demand for Calvert's Isotron products increased rapidly.

And as one participant put it, "I enjoyed the fact that a lot of folks thought it couldn't be done. That's what was best about the hydrofluoric acid effort—beating the old, so-called 'great' production rates."

❯❯ *Breakthrough Project Design*

Let's see how to use each of the five guidelines in selecting projects that are "loaded for success."

1. Focus on an Urgent and Compelling Goal

There is no way to arouse energy and enthusiasm from people who are working on goals they don't feel a sense of urgency about. "Important" and "urgent" are not the same. It may be very important for a company to speed up its pace of bringing new products to market; but the sense of urgency may exist only around a few key products that are being overwhelmed by the competition. Similarly, overall cost reduction may be very important to a company. But no cost reduction program can ever generate a sense of urgency to equal what the Calvert City managers brought to reducing hydrofluoric acid costs, with the "life-and-death" implication for the plant. Any quality improvement project would be focused on an *important* goal; but a breakthrough project focuses on an *urgent* goal.

One final point: while "excellent quality" or "superb customer service" may be urgent goals from top management's point of view, the sense of urgency surrounding a breakthrough goal must be felt by those who must make the project succeed.

2. Set a First-Step Subgoal to Achieve Quickly

Many important business goals are so big, so complex, and so far out in the future, there's almost no hope that they could provide the zest that spontaneously occurs in crisis situations. In order for a goal to be stimulating, its achievement must be within sight. When I first started running, my first target was to do a mile. If I had aimed at competitive marathoning—which became possible much, much later—how long would that goal have sustained me during the early days?

Thus an important part of selecting an achievable breakthrough goal is to stop focusing on the entire situation in all its discouraging complexity and to find a subgoal that you have some chance of accomplishing soon.

A manageable first breakthrough can be extracted from a large, general improvement goal in a number of ways. You can start with one plant, one branch, or one department. Or it might make sense to zero in on one line of business, one category of customers, or even one important customer. Perhaps the project can focus on completing one aspect of a complex organizational change, with other aspects left until later.

Managers are often anxious about focusing this way: what if other performance goes to seed while we concentrate on one goal? Or they worry that the short-term effort may produce no lasting improvement. As we will see later, these fears are ungrounded. By focusing on a discrete first step, managers become able to see much more clearly the linkage between the steps

» The Breakthrough Goal Selection at Calvert City: Narrowing Down to a Short-Term Achievable Result

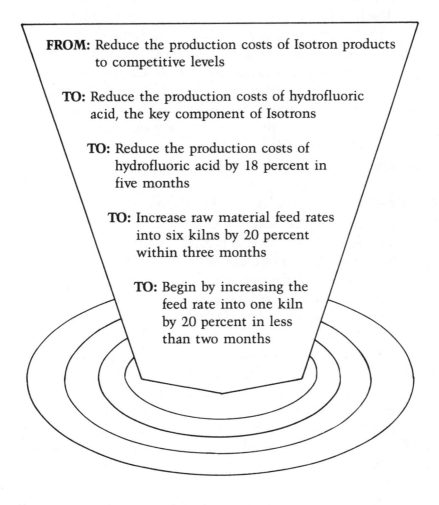

FROM: Reduce the production costs of Isotron products to competitive levels

TO: Reduce the production costs of hydrofluoric acid, the key component of Isotrons

TO: Reduce the production costs of hydrofluoric acid by 18 percent in five months

TO: Increase raw material feed rates into six kilns by 20 percent within three months

TO: Begin by increasing the feed rate into one kiln by 20 percent in less than two months

they must take today and the results they want to achieve tomorrow. As a result, they begin to gain greater control over all their responsibilities.

The management of Motorola's Mobile Division wanted to speed up its new product development process. In this business, which manufactures two-way mobile radios used in trucks, ambulances, police cars, and other vehicles, the development cycle for a new product was typically eighteen months or more. How could the short-term subgoal guideline be applied to such a situation? Some of the most challenging steps of a new product's development came in the final stages—the transfer of the product from the laboratory into full-scale manufacturing of top-quality, reliable products. This division's breakthrough project focused on three products that had fallen behind schedule. The goal was to meet target dates in the final stages of development and introduction for those three products. By focusing the breakthrough project on the final stages of development work, it was possible to achieve a short-term goal as a step in improving product development, which is a long-term process.

3. Make the Breakthrough Goal Bottom-Line and Measurable

To overcome the entrenched "preparations-first" habit and reinforce the "results-first" habit, it is essential that the breakthrough goal be bottom-line and measurable.

If the aim is to improve the quality, then the goal must be an actual reduction of defects or scrap or an actual increase in yields of real products, parts or service. Similarly, in a productivity improvement or cost reduction project, the goal should be a certain number of dollars saved, or units produced, with the same resources. Many managers are so deeply rooted in the preparations-first mentality that, even when they agree to select a "measurable, bottom-line goal," their idea of such a goal is "training a certain number of managers in statistical quality control," or "analyzing the problems of quality on a certain number of parts."

Managers often delay improvement efforts because they are convinced that, if measures of performance are weak or nonexistent, good measures must be created before performance can be improved. The experience of the Philadelphia Electric Company shows that this assumption isn't true. This company took a first step in creating a performance improvement effort with a project in the maintenance area of its highest cost generating station. When asked to select a measurable breakthrough goal, the maintenance supervisors explained that definitive measures of performance did not exist: "So many factors affect our results that it's almost impossible to measure our performance accurately."

The station manager did not want to invest a lot of time and effort establishing a new measurement system—the pressure was on for results. When pressed for more detail, the supervisors acknowledged that basic data was in fact being kept on one aspect of performance: delays in the start-up of scheduled work. When maintenance or repair jobs started later than scheduled, operating equipment and employees, as well as maintenance personnel, sat idle, at great cost to the company.

The plant established a first breakthrough goal of reducing maintenance job start-up delays. This goal required collaboration by the people who operated the equipment. To prevent accidents, no maintenance job could start before the operating people had provided a "job permit" certifying that it would be safe to work on the equipment. Delays in providing these permits were prime culprits in job start-up delays. As soon as permits began being issued on time by operators, maintenance was able to do the rest. Within a few months, they had made a significant reduction in delays. With this start, they then identified some possibilities for staff reduction, and implemented them for savings of over $2 million a year in payments to a maintenance subcontractor. Thus, they were achieving results from the start, and simultaneously, they were able to work on developing the necessary measurements for further progress.

4. Exploit Existing Readiness—Don't Try to Create New Readiness

Once a short-term, zesty, urgent, and achievable goal is in sight, we need to make sure that the participants say, "It's about time we did this," and not, "Oh no. Not this again." Working with people's readiness often does not coincide with the cold logic of technologists or senior management—but it makes for a lot more enthusiasm.

For example, a 20 percent increase in the rate of feed into the kilns was the goal that top management at Calvert City wanted to reach, but they would have agreed to a smaller first step if that was all the team felt they could achieve. Their aim was to generate forward momentum—not to argue over what the ultimate goal ought to be.

To identify readiness, you need to ask the right kinds of questions of the people who are going to be responsible for success. Consider the following approaches to assessing readiness: "There are a number of ways to get started on a goal like this. Which steps do you think will be easiest to take and will have the highest payoff in the shortest amount of time?" Or, "Which steps do you think you can carry out successfully, right now, with the people and resources in place?" These questions keep the focus on the participants themselves and on what they can accomplish, and discourage them from pointing fingers at other people or at outside conditions. In contrast, questions such as, "What do you think has been causing this problem?" or, "What do you think will solve it?" encourage such shifting of responsibility.

Senior managers often worry about limiting improvement goals to only what the participating managers say they are able to achieve. "What happens if the goal they select is too easy?" they ask. That could be a problem if you are setting goals for a year. The advantage of the breakthrough goal is that it is short-term. Zestful success in a short time is the aim, not endless debate about the ultimate "right" goal.

That point was demonstrated dramatically to Francois Fleury, the superintendent of the Mount Wright iron ore complex of USX Corporation's Quebec Cartier Mining Company. Judging from his previous experience, Fleury was certain that the maintenance on the mine's heavy equipment—particularly five "Michigans," huge bulldozers used to move massive rocks—was being done poorly.

Fleury called together the top production and maintenance managers and told them that they had one year to get the Michigans' in-service time from 38 percent up to 65 percent. But after Fleury left the meetings everyone agreed that the goal was impossible. This was reported to Fleury.

At the next meeting with his people, Fleury took a new approach. He asked them what improvement they thought was possible. They said they could probably go from 38 percent to 50 percent in-service time. "I'll agree to that," said Fleury. "We'll set the goal at 50 percent, but you have to get there in four months, not one year." They accepted the challenge.

Organizing the work as a series of breakthrough projects, they reached the 50 percent in-service level by the end of four months. But by that time their confidence had grown. They kept moving on the improvement steps they had inaugurated, and by the end of six months they reached 72 percent, surpassing Fleury's "impossible" one-year goal.

Tom Fogarty, an executive in Chase Manhattan's Metropolitan Community Bank, describes another benefit of step-by-step goal adjustment:

> One of our breakthrough goals was to go from an average downtime of 90 minutes on our automatic teller machines, due to one particular malfunction, to 35 minutes. When we succeeded, we decided to go for 10 minutes as a goal. The team actually got it to 15 minutes, but couldn't cut it down any further. We considered the project a complete success and accepted 15 minutes. After living with 90 minutes for so long, you have to reevaluate what is really achievable and adjust.

5. Use Available Resources and Authority

The perfect excuse for every manager who has failed to meet an expectation is, "I did my part, but . . ." something or someone prevented success. A *Forbes* Magazine reporter asked Roger Smith, chairman of General Motors, why a reorganization to eliminate Fisher Body and the General Motors Assembly Division (GMAD) had been necessary. The reporter asked Smith why he didn't try to solve the problems by calling in the boss of Fisher Body and saying, "If I get one more complaint about your division, you and the top three guys are finished." Smith responded:

> Okay, we could do that, and it's the way we used to do it. But he [the Fisher man] says, "Wait a minute. I did my job. My job was to fabricate a steel door, and I made a steel door, and I shipped it to GMAD. And it's GMAD's fault." So you go over to the GMAD guy and say: "Listen, one more lousy door and you're fired." He says, "Wait a minute, I took what Fisher gave me and the car division's specs and I put them togehter, so it's not my fault." So you get the Chevrolet guy, and you say, "One more

lousy door, and . . ." "Wait a minute," he says. "All I got is what GMAD made." So pretty soon you're back to the Fisher guy, and all you are doing is running around in great big circles.

Every president has spent endless hours in such conversations. In launching a breakthrough project, a new message is delivered: each of us will begin accomplishing what can be accomplished by ourselves with whatever is at hand—and we're going to start right now. We are not going to select a goal that requires changes by another department (unless they indicate that they are willing collaborators in the project). We will not select a goal that requires additional people or additional equipment or additional space or new systems or measurements. Nor will we select a goal that requires senior management to excuse us from another commitment, or a goal we can achieve only after some other function has accomplished its goal.

The shutting down of these escape routes requires a firm weaning away from the comfortable patterns of rationalization. The Bonaventure terminal managers provide a clear example of this shift. Since their transportation department always delivered their box cars late, they protested, how could the terminal itself improve service? Every manager who attempts to achieve performance improvement meets this kind of rejoinder. The way to respond is not to challenge the validity of such protests. You must ask this kind of question: "Is there anything, *anything at all*, that can be done within the department itself to improve reliability?" The answer that almost always comes back is, "Well, maybe a few things." That is where to begin. Once people are willing to give up the security blanket of, "It can't be done until . . . ," a transformation has begun. It may be a mere spark—but it has the potential to ignite a raging brushfire of progress.

"Pick a Winner"

The breakthrough strategy advises managers to bypass all of the preparations and excuses and to get going directly, at once, toward a short-term result, a success. The aim is to permit managers and their people to enjoy the same soul-satisfying, empowering, zestful experience that they typically enjoy only in those rare moments of crisis when everyone pitches in to achieve an urgent result. The breakthrough project is a liberating experience because it can provide, in an orderly and controlled fashion, a breakthrough to a new level of achievement and a new way of working.

6

>> Use Each Success to Develop Performance Capability

It is a great experience for managers who haven't tasted much success to participate in a successful breakthrough project. One success, however—no matter how gratifying it may be—is of little lasting value unless it is the beginning of something that continues.

Many managers report: "When we're in a jam, we can really get things done here. People go like there's no tomorrow. But once the job gets done, they fall back. You can't keep it going." That's precisely the challenge that managers want answers to—how to "keep it going." In the Pennwalt Calvert City plant, increasing the rate of feeding materials into a single kiln was the initial project; but it was the many projects that followed that reduced the cost of Pennwalt's product to competitive levels.

It is only by infusing each short-term success with developmental elements that the capacity for sustained progress is created. It is the combination of *success* and *development* that makes the breakthrough strategy so powerful.

What are these developmental elements? They are a few familiar, rudimentary practices, virtually the ABCs of management. Most managers assume they carry out these practices well; in fact, they are done very poorly in a great many companies.

There is nothing new about these practices, or management precepts. Chester Barnard, Peter Drucker, and other management thinkers were writing about them many years ago. In fact, many managers feel patronized by the suggestion that these are the keys to increasing their capacity to achieve results. "We do all those things," they say. "We have all those basics under control." When you begin to probe, however, it becomes evident that most organizations, as described in Chapter 2, have big gaps in these basic work elements.

›› The Keys to the Kingdom

This chapter will help you recognize the great benefits that can come from more effective use of these powerful, well-established precepts of good management. The key to making every breakthrough project a vehicle for strengthening the organization's basic performance capability is to build into each project a more sophisticated application of the following six precepts. Is this a plea for going "back to basics?" No. For most of us, it is a case of forging "ahead to basics."

›› The Keys to the Kingdom

1. Individual Accountability for Results
2. Clear-cut Demand-Making
3. Written Work Plans and Reviews of Progress
4. Structured Involvement of Those With Contributions to Make
5. Testing of Innovative Approaches
6. Frequent Reinforcement and Rewards

---

1. Individual Accountability Is Real Accountability

In modern organizations, almost every significant change or improvement requires input from people located in different parts of the organization. It is easy for managers in charge of projects to rationalize that they are doing everything that needs to be done, within the limitations of their jobs. Then when a project fails, each of the participating managers can assert that his or her part was well done. From these individual assessments, it is just a short step to the business unit whose top managers were all rated "above average" or "outstanding," but which was losing money.

When a breakthrough goal is selected, I always ask the senior manager, "Who is going to be accountable for the results?" I am usually given the names of a number of people. When I ask for the designation of *one* person, I am told it is impossible to name one because several groups have important roles.

A critical development step, therefore, is to make one manager fully accountable for each goal and subgoal, no matter where the resources may be located. Accepting that kind of accountability will be new for most managers. That's why it is a "breakthrough." Assigning full accountability will teach managers—so many of whom have never learned this—what it means to be responsible for producing the ultimate result, rather than for merely doing their part of the job.

The crucial task of new product development provides innumerable opportunities for divided accountability because it involves nearly every function in the company: specifying what that new product is to be, designing it, moving it into manufacture, and eventually pricing, promoting, and selling it profitably. Most often, each function is carried out within the boundaries of departments; when a product is late or fails, nobody is responsible because every department "did its job."

The shift to individual accountability seems so simple in concept, and yet it profoundly affects the way managers view their tasks. Individual employees continue to be responsible for their own work, much as they had been before; but when there is a problem to be dealt with on a particular product, there is no doubt about who to call. Only one person is responsible. An accountable manager can no longer "explain" why a project did not meet its goals. Success or failure simply cannot be ascribed to others.

2. Demand Better Results—and Get Them

The most weakly developed skill of managers is the capacity to ask for better performance in ways that win commitment and achieve results. We highlighted in Chapter 2 some of the ways by which managers allow themselves to think they are asking for improved results, but are actually missing the mark. Because the breakthrough project is so well-defined, so short-term, and so focused, it permits managers to observe with unusual clarity the demand/response patterns between themselves and their people. And because it is loaded for success, the breakthrough project offers a low-risk vehicle for testing how to strengthen that interaction.

Once the general nature of the initial breakthrough goal is defined, the first step is to work out with the one accountable manager, and possibly the other key players, the precise goal that is to be achieved.

The Bonaventure Terminal case provides a good example. The express superintendent for the St. Lawrence region had constantly told the managers of the terminal to improve service, meet the delivery time schedules, reduce costs, and improve employee relations. When he wanted to be "tough," he would pound the table or send out veiled threats. His managers rarely met these goals, and he rarely let much time pass before reminding them of their failures. In doing so, he saw himself as a conscientious manager being clear with his people about what was expected of them. He did not realize the significance of the pattern he had fallen into: He stated the expectations. The managers did not meet them. In response, he did little more than restate the expectations. After a few times around on that merry-go-round, both he and his people fully understood that his demands carried little weight.

It was only when the terminal managers committed themselves to a very specific, short-term improvement, focused on one train, that the nature of the dialogue shifted significantly. His request and their response suddenly were tied to real, measurable performance; they were all freed from the old charade. "Success" had a date and a number and a *commitment* attached to it.

The next step is to work with the accountable manager (or managers, if there are several subprojects) to make sure that all of the possible "escape hatches" are closed off. For example, because the goal is relatively near-term, the parties agree that they will not allow "changing conditions" during the course of the project to influence their ability to achieve it.

No matter how modest an improvement the breakthrough goal may be, it can serve as a hammer to break the mold of weak or ambiguous demand-making. It gives the manager who initiates the process experience in being really clear with a subordinate about what must be achieved and in making sure that the subordinate understands that commitment. This clarity and the unambiguous nature of the commitment are as significant as any other dimensions of the breakthrough project.

3. Written Work Planning to Discipline Management Work

As demand-making becomes sharper and accountability more clear-cut, work planning disciplines provide additional guarantees that the breakthrough goals will be achieved. The two critical elements in the work planning disciplines are (1) written project assignments that define those goals to be achieved, and (2) written work plans that outline how the goals will be achieved.

Project Assignments.
The project assignment is generally in the form of a memorandum from senior management to the manager (or managers) who will be accomplishing the goal. The project assignment describes the goal and explains how the goal fits into the overall strategic thrust of the organization.

In *The Practice of Management*, Peter Drucker recounts the story of the stonemasons who were asked what they were doing. One said, "I am making a living." The second responded, "I am doing the best job of stonecutting in the country." The third responded, "I'm building a cathedral." While the second mason's concern for quality is an improvement over the narrow vision of the first, it does not go far enough. It is also important for the stonemasons to share a vision of the cathedral they are building. In launching a major improvement effort, the breakthrough project assignment can be used to share perspective about the ultimate goals to which the project is a contribution.

When the Philadelphia Electric Company launched the cost reduction program in its maintenance function, management established the context for the first breakthroughs in the project assignment memo below. Of course, such letters are not fired off in isolation; there is considerable discussion among the managers involved. When agreements are reached, the project assignment is written—to nail down for the record what goal was agreed to and what must be done next.

PROJECT ASSIGNMENT

❯❯ *Philadelphia Electric Company*

From: R. W. Helt—Station Superintendent
To: Shift Superintendent and Plant Engineers

Beginning today we are going to work on reducing delays in maintenance projects due to late completion of permits. I am taking the following steps:

1. I am instituting a policy of two-day advanced notice for permits required. This means that all operating shifts will have two days to complete their assigned permits instead of the current 24 hours. With more time to plan and carry out the blocking of equipment in preparation for maintenance work, each shift should increase its percentage of blocks completed when requested.

2. I am asking Walt Masny to take the lead in a three-month project to measure permit delays and institute steps to reduce the delays. Walt will select a goal, set up a work program to measure actual completion rates, delays, and causes of delays, and report back to me each day with results. He will also be calling upon you and the maintenance organization to devise new procedures, new methods—whatever is needed to reduce delays—and to thereby help us improve the utilization of our maintenance forces. I've asked Walt for a plan and progress report within one month.

This is a pilot breakthrough project for the Eddystone Station. E. J. Onley, Manager of Hydro-Fossil Production, has asked us to take this step as part of the department's effort to improve output through better utilization of resources we have, rather than through additional investments in equipment and staff.

Sometimes managers even ask a subordinate to write a draft of the assignment to himself—for the manager's signature—as a way of testing the subordinate's understanding.

Work Plans.

A work plan is an action blueprint describing how the break-through goal, which was defined in the project assignment, will actually be accomplished. It usually includes the following elements:

1. A statement of the goal, together with any necessary background information
2. A list of the specific tasks to be accomplished or steps to be carried out
3. Who is to be responsible for each task or step
4. The timetable, including start and completion dates for each task or step
5. Measures and/or indices of progress (sometimes called milestones) that will serve as clear evidence of the accomplishment of each task
6. A specific description of the method for reviewing progress periodically

During the performance improvement effort at Philadelphia Electric, a maintenance department team developed the work plan shown on the next page, to accomplish a subgoal.

It is important that all of the parties who have a role to play in carrying out the work plan actually participate in its creation. I have seen work plans that were computerized and printed in four colors, using the most elaborate software, but because the contracting parties had not really worked out ac-countabilities and had not discussed the realities of the steps to be taken, the plans were not worth the paper they were printed on. A plan on the back of an envelope that everybody under-stands and is dedicated to making succeed is much more valu-able than a pile of computer printouts that do not have the real commitment of participants.

When a breakthrough project is launched, the planning for it should include the scheduling of periodic progress reviews. These should not be ad hoc sessions called only if it is suspected that the project is in trouble. The reviews give participating managers the chance to test progress against plans and to assess whether any changes should be made on the basis of experience

>> *Work Plan*

Date Prepared: _____10/14_____
Revised: _____10/30_____

GOAL: Complete one extra job per day per pipe fitter without increasing cost per job, in 10 weeks (1/1/87).

(Include *what* will be achieved; *how* it will *measured; target date*)

Prime Responsbility of: Jack Campbell

#	Steps (Start each with action verb)	Who* Resp.	Target Dates Beg.	End	Result or Output	Status As Of: 10/30
1	*Create measurement system*: Calculate historical cost per job to define baseline measure	Bob Matty Bill Bergem	10/14	10/18	Graph of cost per job	Being plotted
2	Develop computer report of actual hours per completed job each week	Jack Camp	10/16	11/3	Report developed and available	Done 10/29
3	*Make changes in work procedures*: Ensure equipment blocked within half-hour of scheduled maintenance	Walt Masney Shift Supt.	10/20	10/30	No delays greater than one-half hour	Open 10/30
4	Formalize process to schedule and issue extra jobs	Jack C. Walt M.	10/20	11/7	Process outlined	Open 10/30
5	Formalize procedure for giving extra work to vendor	Jack C.	10/14	10/30	Process outlined	Open 10/30
6	Create new category of work: "No block required, do anytime"	E. Welch	10/20	10/30	New work category utilized	Open 10/30
7	*Perform involvement action steps*: Meeting with shift supervisors to issue project guidelines	Jack C.	10/21	10/21	Guidelines issued	Done 10/21
8	Kickoff meeting with supervisors and fitters	Jack C.	10/24	10/24	Fitters clear on goal and plan	Done 10/24
9	*Evaluate progress*: Determine number of satisfactory jobs completed at base-line cost	Jack C.	12/1	1/1	Number of extra jobs completed known	Open 10/30
10	Determine reduction of vendor manpower	Al Elmy	12/1	1/1	Backlog of fitter work reviewed	Open 10/30

*If more than one person is responsible for a step, circle who has prime responsbility.
© Robert H. Schaffer & Associates

thus far. The senior manager can find out quickly and efficiently what is happening and can decide whether any interventions are needed.

A well-written work plan provides the structure for these reviews. Key players can report on the progress of each subproject. The meeting can concentrate on elements that have fallen behind schedule: What changes do you need to make in the plan? What would help get the project back on track?

In the early 1980s, Lloyd Spalter, a Uniroyal executive, was given the unenviable task of presiding over the company's footware division, which was in difficulty and in danger of being sold off. With the Keds brand name, the division had once been at the top of the heap. But as the athletic footware business began its dramatic upward move, the Uniroyal operation was heading in the opposite direction.

When Spalter took over, the division was preparing for its yearly new product launch—in a most disorganized fashion. It appeared that many samples were not going to be ready on time. Coordination among the key groups was spotty. Yet just a few months away in August, the entire sales force was scheduled to come together to see the new fall product line. It was the most critical meeting of the year.

Spalter realized he would have to work fast to avoid disaster. He called his people together and organized a series of break-through projects, each of them focused on achieving one of the tasks essential to having the full line ready for the launch meeting. He also announced that until that date, the entire group was to meet every Friday morning at 8:00 a.m. to review the projects. "That's when we begin," said Spalter. "We'll end when we're finished."

At first, most of the group had written off his declarations as "just more smoke." But projects were organized; work plans were shared; and within a week or two, people began to realize that Spalter was serious about meeting the goal. Each Friday every subproject was reviewed. Those that were on target might occupy ten or twenty minutes of the agenda. Those that were in trouble occupied as much time as it took to reach agreements. It was in those meetings that everyone gradually realized not only that Spalter was serious, but also that he might have a fighting chance of making his goal.

And he did make it. Moreover, even though virtually everyone was demoralized by the suspicion that the division was up for sale, the kickoff meeting and the work that went into preparing the launch inspired the sales force so much that, after several years of steadily declining sales, they actually sold more during the fall campaign than they had the previous year.

4. Structured Involvement of Those With Contributions to Make

When describing zestful situations, people almost always mention that when results must be achieved, the organization's traditional operational and hierarchical boundary lines evaporate. People group themselves as necessary to get the job done. A breakthrough project stimulates this same process.

Too many employee involvement efforts, like those described in Chapter 3, are hothouse activities in which employees are brought together in a sanitized atmosphere and management, somewhat like indulgent parents, encourages them to say their piece. Involvement in a breakthrough project—like collaboration in a crisis—takes place in an environment in which the urgent goal to be achieved is the focal point. People are brought together because they have meaningful contributions to make—based on their knowledge, not their status—not because it is nice to have "employee involvement."

For example, at the Aliquippa, Pennsylvania mill of Jones & Laughlin Steel Company, a task team was assembled to eliminate the misidentification of steel bars and rods, which had resulted in customers receiving incorrect shipments. Because several union employees had unique knowledge of the identification and record-keeping processes, they were invited to serve on the task team along with management members. It was a most logical decision, but it was a major innovation for the company. The contributions of these two employees were vital to the project's success—a significant, measurable reduction in misidentified steel and a major improvement in customer assessment of the company's quality.

It can be threatening to some managers when people move freely across functions or skip levels and go directly to those with the information, and when more attention is paid to what people can contribute than to their levels or titles. After all, many of the hierarchical protocols in organizations have been established as much to make managers feel secure as to get work accomplished. The breakthrough project can begin to dissolve these rigid constraints. The project manager should be encouraged to draw in as active participants all who have a role to play, without regard to boundaries or structure.

The incremental nature of the breakthrough projects permits managers to experiment, one safe step at a time, with new modes for successfully bringing together people who can achieve the result—without being overly threatened about the erosion of their authority.

When bringing different levels and groups together to work on joint projects, it is important to spell out clearly the roles and responsibilities of each. Companies devote much time and attention to their formal organization charts and job descriptions. Yet so much of the really important work gets done in groups that come together temporarily, with no clear job definitions in their working relationships. The breakthrough project offers the opportunity to introduce the use of temporary formal organization charts and job definitions by developing them for projects with finite lives. These temporary charts and job descriptions define the work arrangements of the project. They assure consensus and clarity about who will be held responsible for accomplishing the overall goal and its subparts; the nature of relationships between all involved; and their individual roles and functions. Even if these temporary structures last only a few months, during their brief existence they provide guidance for the most important innovations and initiatives of the enterprise.

5. Low-Risk Testing of Innovative Approaches

Breakthrough projects, because they are self-contained and low-risk, provide a protected environment for the testing of innovations. Moreover, the short-term focus of the projects makes it possible to get fast feedback on whether the innovations are accomplishing what they are supposed to.

The manager of a Lever Brothers plant once complained to me that he had tried unsuccessfully to obtain approval for installing ten new converters for the processing of detergents. The converters would pay for themselves within two or three years, thus generating enormous cost savings as well as improved quality. He had submitted a capital appropriation request for $1.5 million several years in a row. But each year, the appropriation was turned down.

I asked him to identify the corporate managers who would have to approve the $1.5 million request and to speculate on what their individual views might be about his justification numbers. He reluctantly reported what we both already knew—that the plant's credibility was not high. No matter how compelling the numbers, they would not be taken as gospel truth.

"Why not put in a request for one converter at $150,000?" I asked, "Try it out, and then you'll have results to show." He snapped back that other companies had used the converters, and the numbers were so compelling that my suggested approach seemed ridiculous. He displayed the resistance that managers often show to a step-at-a-time testing of innovation. The approach seems "too slow." But since the all-or-nothing approach wasn't working, he requested $150,000 and got it. Much more work than he had anticipated was required to make the equipment work properly, but eventually it proved out. The numbers were as convincing as he had said they would be, and there was no problem getting the other nine converters on the next budget go-around.

Every breakthrough project could include some innovative steps that can be tested like this on a low-risk basis.

6. Reinforcements and Rewards

Most jobs give people dismally few opportunities to be heroines or heroes, to feel like winners and be seen as winners. Their work lives are a dreary routine of repetitive tasks as they move from one project to the next, one chore to the next, one monthly report to the next. In contrast, one short-term breakthrough project following another gives people many more opportunities to feel like winners.

In citing the zest factors, managers always point up that emergency situations really motivate people to show that they can do it, that they can rise to the challenge and succeed. There is a sense of drama. Anyone who watches a Superbowl or other championship game can't help but notice how much the locker room of the winning team differs from that of the losing team. Success is exhilarating, defeat frustrating. Yet executives, who as spectators may witness such scenes repeatedly, usually fail utterly to apply this lesson to the people working for them.

>> Key Ingredients of a Breakthrough Project

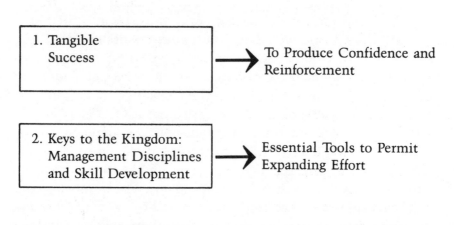

1. Tangible Success	→ To Produce Confidence and Reinforcement
2. Keys to the Kingdom: Management Disciplines and Skill Development	→ Essential Tools to Permit Expanding Effort

To enhance the momentum generated by success in breakthrough projects, deliberate steps should be taken to make heroes of the participants. The design of breakthrough projects, with clear-cut beginnings and ends, work plans, measurements, and reviews, makes it easy to provide frequent, positive feedback. The following example from a project at the Chase Manhattan Bank illustrates several ways to do so.

The "lockbox unit" of the bank serves companies—like large public utilities—that receive a large number of monthly payments. Instead of going directly to the utility, customer payments go to the 100-person lockbox unit, which processes them directly into the utility's account.

Although the unit was handling hundreds of thousands of transactions with a high degree of accuracy, enough errors were being made to generate concern. An overall goal was established to improve accuracy by 50 percent within five months. This goal was then divided into shorter term subgoals. Managers organized a series of breakthrough projects under several supervisors.

As the project got underway, a three-by-five-foot chart was posted showing progress on the projects. Each week, results were recorded. As steps were implemented, the decreasing error level became clearly visible. It also became a frequent topic of conversation in the department. When the goal was successfully reached, the unit's manager described the project in presentations to groups of higher level managers. As a result, some senior managers visited the unit, presented awards, and offered their congratulations. The lockbox unit had been transformed into a model of success.

The use of wall charts or published charts is but one way to reinforce the success experiences of a project. Other managers take groups out to dinner. Seeing the project manager late at night delivering pizzas and soft drinks to the workers on the Motorola pager project was an unforgettable moment for them. Company periodicals can effectively recognize the "winners" and spread breakthrough strategy concepts.

» Provident Mutual Insurance Company

Just as the insidious barriers mutually reinforce each other, so the management practices introduced during a breakthrough project reinforce each other in accelerating performance. This is well illustrated by the experience of Provident Mutual, where many of these disciplines helped to organize a critical breakthrough project.

In the summer of 1986, the Provident Mutual Insurance Company in Philadelphia decided to develop the most sophisticated product in the history of the company. It was called "Intersector-Plus," and it was to be the life insurance policy that would "never have to be replaced" because of its enormous flexibility in coverages, premium rates, cash values, and optional benefits. The new policy was expected to constitute a large percentage of the business to be written in 1987—the very next year—even though a recently introduced and a less complex variable life insurance policy had taken them almost two years to develop.

Traditionally, the actuarial function was the driving force for developing and introducing new products at Provident, as it is at other life insurance companies. The actuaries would come up with a product idea, in collaboration with marketing people. They would ask the legal department to make applications to various states to obtain approvals for the new product. They would ask Marketing to prepare product announcements, sales strategies, and training for field agents. They would orient the operations group to the new product and request that they train their people to administer it. They would ask Systems to build the administrative software to manage the new product. This last step was the most complex. Frequently, the original systems designs had to be modified as the product was refined and tested against the legal requirements of the states where the policy was to be sold. It was normal for this iterative process to take many months.

Although initiated by the actuaries, the development of new products typically had been a cooperative venture among functions, without sharp accountability for results. Because of the importance of Intersector-Plus, a strong central project manager was essential. David Warner, the vice president of underwriting, was appointed project manager with accountability for delivering a successful product (Key No. 1: individual accountability).

In November of 1986, Bob Gibbons, Provident's senior vice president for individual insurance, and Dave Warner's boss, set a target date for Intersector-Plus introduction of the following July 1—just eight months away—to hit the market at mid-year, during the peak selling period (Key No. 2: clear-cut demand-making). A competitor had already spent about eighteen months developing a similar product.

Dave Warner and the others involved took a deep breath. With accountability fixed on Warner and the demand from Gibbons clearly stated, the key players met to see how to apply the other other breakthrough strategy "keys to the kingdom," to help make success possible.

They defined "successful introduction" of Intersector-Plus more specifically as: (1) legal approval by next July 1 in any four out of the six key states in the country; (2) by July 1, field agents trained and ready to sell, systems up and running to process initial applications, and advertising and communications materials in place; and (3) by October, legal approval in a minimum of forty states overall.

An advisory committee was created consisting of the vice presidents of all the functions that would contribute to the project. The committee, plus Dave Warner and the key people who would manage each part of the program, became an organized group with the sole purpose of launching Intersector-Plus (Key No. 4: structured involvement).

Dave Warner created a master plan for the entire project, with a sketch of what each function would have to accomplish. Functional groups formerly working essentially in isolation now submitted plans to dovetail with this overall plan (Key No. 3: written work plans). Warner then presented the master plan to the advisory committee, which approved it. Bob Gibbons took the bold step of announcing to the field force that the home office would deliver the Intersector-Plus product on 1 July 1987, then just seven months away.

The project's first subgoal was to complete a detailed product specification manual so that Systems could design the systems right the first time and minimize recycling. Actuaries and marketing people worked together intensively for three weeks, and a huge document far more detailed than any previous product specification was prepared. This first target date was met with success.

Next, all of the other project elements were defined as discrete subprojects with specified beginnings and ends. Project managers were assigned to see that each subproject met its target dates. Warner held joint review meetings with the subproject managers each Wednesday morning at breakfast and met with them individually when necessary. They exchanged progress reports, picked up loose ends, and coordinated actions (Key No. 3: review of progress).

In previous product developments, hundreds of Provident Mutual people had been "involved," but with little sense of collaboration. During the development of Intersector-Plus, the regular involvement of the subproject managers on Dave Warner's core team kept every function actively wired in. Over forty people were directly involved, and hundreds of others contributed (Key No. 4: structured involvement). The advisory committee met with Warner and the managers every two weeks in regular review sessions. The company's communications department covered the story in the company newspaper, describing how the project was advancing and explaining the product's significance to the company (Key No. 6: frequent reinforcement).

In the past, people had been splintered among many projects and had to make time allocation decisions on their own. This time, commitments were negotiated "in public" to ensure that adequate resources would be put on Intersector-Plus and to obtain agreement on adjusted target dates for other projects. Top-management commitment kept every function aware of the top-priority status of the project.

The tight deadlines stimulated a major innovation in securing approvals of Intersector-Plus by state insurance regulatory agencies. To make sure there would be no hitches when the applications were submitted, the actuarial and law departments teamed up to conduct "presubmission visits" in important states such as California, New York, New Jersey, Pennsylvania, and Massachusetts. They briefed key people on the new product and found out what might be necessary to win approval. The law department also established an information system to track its submissions to state agencies so that it could shepherd the submissions through the approval process, rather than just wait for approvals (Key No. 5: testing of innovative approaches). By July 1, over thirty states had approved the new insurance product.

As the end of June approached, the marketing department capped the whole effort with a teleconference that introduced

Intersector-Plus to the entire nationwide agency force in one dramatic event (Key No. 5 again: testing another innovation).

Dave Warner reflected on how everyone had worked together: "It's amazing to discover what we really are capable of doing." By July 1, field agents already had applications out, and within weeks applications for insurance were being processed and revenues generated. It had taken Provident Mutual just over eight months to develop and introduce the product.

Success as the Launching Pad

Thus we see how the breakthrough strategy begins to shift the organization's basic performance capability. It allows managers to break through in two ways. The first is a breakthrough to a new level of achievement. The second, is a breakthrough in management methodology for accomplishing results. The breakthrough project serves as a vehicle for introducing new patterns of work, essential management practices, and new sophistication in organizing for accomplishment.

The reinforcement of success, and the repeated use of new methods in achieving that success create a powerful learning experience. By these means, the first one or two breakthrough projects can become the foundation upon which to build an accelerating and expanding process of improvement.

7

>> *Widening the Circle of Success*

The tangible successes of the initial breakthrough projects reinforce the confidence of managers who have carried them out. These managers have penetrated the barriers in their own organizations to produce significant bottomline gains. In doing so, they have sharpened and reinforced critical skills and work practices. But that is just the beginning of the story; the stage is now set for moving on.

>> *Success as the Springboard to More Success*

As manager of Data Operations for Metropolitan Community Bank (Chase Manhattan Bank's network of branches in metropolitan New York), Tom Fogarty was responsible for providing a wide range of computer support for all branch functions. He also oversaw the performance and servicing of more than 200 automatic teller machines (ATMs). When he finished reviewing some very detailed plans to consolidate his two computer centers into one, he was really pleased. The two computer centers in Lake Success, New York, had been in separate organizations under different managers, and their consolidation would save over $1.5 million in equipment and operational costs in

1987. Fogarty congratulated his project manager, Frank Oberster, on the completeness of the consolidation plans. What pleased him so much was that the planning was not only well done, but it had been relatively *easy*!

He thought back to the year before and shook his head. "We couldn't even have considered this project then," he said. "Get our daily work done while completely reorganizing our operations? It would have taken me two weeks just to get people together into a room to talk about it."

One year earlier, in 1986, Fogarty had launched a first breakthrough project to improve ATM performance. The ATM network is highly visible, and as anyone who has urgently needed $50 on a Sunday morning knows, it definitely affects perceptions of a bank's quality of service. Previous efforts had improved the performance record of Chase's ATMs, but the machines were still out of service more often than was acceptable.

The project began with an effort to carve off from the broad general goal—98 percent availability of ATMs—a more specific breakthrough goal. It wasn't easy. Maintaining the widely dispersed ATM network was a complicated business. Using data showing that 85 percent of the machine failures were not caused by mechanical defects, two breakthrough subteams each selected one of these "simpler" types of failure to correct:

1. Failures caused by customers' errors, including—if you can believe it—forgetting to remove cash from the dispenser drawer. Their breakthrough goal was to reduce such failures at the thirty worst sites by 30 percent in a month.
2. Cash dispenser failures caused, for example, by sticky or crumpled bills. The goal was to reduce these failures 30 percent systemwide within a month.

The improvement initiatives took many forms. ATM software was rewritten to prompt customers more clearly at each step in their transactions; maintenance procedures were improved; one team identified what made the top ten performing branches so successful and applied the lessons throughout the network. One of the two goals was reached on time, and the other just after the deadline.

This first step-up in performance gave Tom Fogarty hints of what might be possible. He was determined to keep going. He established some next-step goals for the original two projects and some new goals as well—for example, to bring the ATM availability rate for the ten worst performing branches up to at least 90 percent.

Simply expanding on the goals of the first breakthrough project is the most straightforward way to multiply and spread the breakthrough successes. Let's follow the story as we identify the various avenues for improvement followed at Metropolitan Community Bank. We'll also see how other managers have reaped a harvest of expanding performance improvement following initial breakthrough successes.

» Breakthrough Multiplication Routes

There are six "multiplication routes"—ways to move from the first success to the next and then the next.

1. Extending the Scope of the Original Breakthrough

As Tom Fogarty showed in going from one improvement in ATM reliability to the next, managers can build on their initial breakthroughs by extending them to longer term or more ambitious goals.

Similarly, in Pennwalt's Calvert City plant, the first goal was to increase raw material feed rates into one kiln. Then the work was extended to include the other kilns. At the Bonaventure Terminal in Montreal, the first breakthrough focused on loading the traffic more efficiently on one particular train. As success was achieved, a number of additional trains were simultaneously targeted for improved results.

As managers develop confidence in themselves and in the breakthrough strategy, they will be more willing to apply it to goals that carry higher stakes.

2. Organizing a Series of New, Related Projects

In addition to expanding on the original projects, the ATM group also went on to target a new aspect of the ATM network. They set a goal for reducing the response time to failures between the machines and the main computer center. The average downtime after such failures had been one hour. The new target was thirty-five minutes.

This illustrates the second breakthrough expansion possibility: to organize a series of new projects related in purpose to the original breakthrough, but involving additional people or functions or tackling a new dimension of the improvement challenge.

» Breakthrough Multiplication Routes

"E Unum Pluribus"

1. Extend the Scope of Original Breakthrough
2. Organize a Series of New Related Projects
3. Move Up and Down the Line
4. Cross Boundaries—Interfunctional Projects
5. Expand by Migration to New Sites
6. Expand Beyond the Gates—to Customers and Vendors

This multiplication approach was used in the Cleveland office of Ameritech Publishing, Inc. (API), where Yellow Pages directories are produced for the state of Ohio. API's Directory Service Bureau is responsible for ensuring that every single piece of advertiser paperwork—both contracts and actual advertising copy—is complete and errorfree.

In 1986, the bureau was grappling with a two-month backlog of work that was overwhelming it and threatening to delay publishing dates. Despite their best efforts, the bureau employees had not been able to reduce the backlog; they saw themselves as lacking the power to influence the situation. Once they were persuaded to attempt it, however, they set an ambitious breakthrough goal of reducing the backlog by 50 percent within one month. Among other actions, they eliminated unnecessary documentation done by the clerks, redesigned the supervisors' jobs, and developed a system for scheduling the work flow into their department. With simple changes like these, plus their own determination, they slashed the backlog.

Once the Directory Service Bureau showed what could be done, projects were launched in other API departments that were coping with backlogs that threatened publishing deadlines. The art and editing department—where advertisements were designed and executed—and the national yellow pages department, which handled large corporate accounts, both set backlog reduction breakthrough goals and achieved them by redesigning work flows, streamlining communications between departments, and resolving long-standing problems with computer systems.

3. Moving Up and Down the Line

As successes are achieved at one level of the organization, they can be spread upward and downward to any other level. At API, the breakthrough teams originally consisted only of supervisors. As the improvement work expanded, groups of clerks were asked to take responsibility for setting and reaching backlog reduction goals by improving their own work methods.

Similarly, soon after the breakthroughs in ATM perform-ance, Tom Fogarty asked each of the five managers reporting to him to define and manage a breakthrough project to improve critical performance in their areas.

4. Crossing Organization Boundaries: Interfunctional Projects

Although a company's initial breakthrough projects can involve a number of functions (as did the Provident Mutual case described in the previous chapter), most begin in one area, where it is easier to mobilize the resources necessary to have a success. Expanding from these one-department breakthroughs usually requires the crossing of functional boundaries. When those boundaries are crossed by groups that have already had their own success, the other functions are more likely to welcome such crossings.

As mentioned earlier, the Bonaventure Terminal managers had always been certain that their service problems were caused by the transportation department's late delivery of the trains. Every conversation they had with the transportation people car-ried the implicit accusation, "If you guys would do your jobs, we could get top management off our backs." That message is a provocation that begs for counterattack. Consider the difference when, after achieving some significant results, terminal managers went to the transportation department to report on their progress and to ask for some support in their further steps. This owning-up to the fact that they themselves had been part of the problem opened the minds of the transportation department's managers to the possibility of collaboration.

At API, supervisors in the Directory Service Bureau had for years felt certain that their severe backlog problem was caused largely by the work flow between their department and the sales function. Sales orders arrived in huge batches at unpredictable intervals. Many of the orders were incomplete or unclear. Salespeople were often hard to reach and seemed uncooperative when asked to provide missing customer information. But salespeople were out working diligently to compete for business advertising dollars and were reluctant to spend more time on clerical chores. It was only after the Directory Service Bureau had been successful at reducing the backlog by improving their own work processes that they could talk to sales without accusations. Only then did the sales unit open up to the possibility of some joint efforts.

At Chase Manhattan Data Operations Department, an interfunctional effort was needed to sustain the early gains. Fogarty's people were able to significantly reduce ATM failures which were preventable by the local branch personnel. But a week after the breakthrough team had officially completed its work and proudly announced its success, the gains began to erode. The team realized that this erosion had occurred because the people who had to sustain the performance improvements—the bank's branch managers—had not been sufficiently involved in the process of achieving them. To save their hard-won gains, the data operations managers established a temporary team, called the ATM User Committee, to help the regional branch managers take responsibiltity for maintaining high standards of ATM availability. Because of their own success, Fogarty's managers could go with proof in hand that their suggested performance levels were indeed reasonable.

They also used a multifunction team in a breakthrough project to merge a small computer center into one of the two large centers, with no interruption in service, for a $200,000 annual cost savings. Interfunctional teams took responsibility for planning and implementing every aspect of this successful merger.

This complicated, but relatively modest, effort was an ideal warm-up for the consolidation of the two large data operations. Gazing down at the detailed consolidation plans in his hands, Fogarty reflected on the series of successful experiences.

> It took a year to get to the point where we could take on a large project like this without much anxiety. Of course, we used to plan the tasks required to reach a goal, but there was never great confidence that we could make it happen. Now we know exactly where we're going, and we know exactly how to get there.

After five months of hard work, the cut-over to a single consolidated center occurred at 12:27 a.m. on November 8, 1987. It had been scheduled for midnight, but perfection always takes a bit longer.

5. Expanding by Migration to New Sites

When successes have been achieved in one major unit of an organization, it is natural for senior management to start the process in other locations. The Metropolitan Community Bank projects took place after about fifteen other functions at Chase Manhattan had successfully employed the breakthrough strategy.

At Atlas Steels, the original work began in a stainless steel mill in Tracey, Quebec. Because the breakthrough strategy had helped that plant go from a loss to a significant profit, the works manager, Guenther Feucht, decided to try it at the new Welland, Ontario melt shop. When the strategy helped to get production up to target there, Feucht then applied it to a plant that performed finishing operations on steel products. The breakthrough projects in that plant increased their on-time delivery rate of finished steel products from 65 percent to 80 percent within a few months.

6. Expanding Beyond the Gates—to Customers and Vendors

The experimental, low-risk nature of the breakthrough strategy has encouraged many managers to reach out and engage customers, suppliers, and distributors in joint breakthrough projects.

Tom Fogarty's people worked with their outside contractor to reduce the costs of maintaining their network of ATMs. Fogarty let the contractor know that he wanted a $300,000 reduction in the next maintenance contract, and that he was looking into other vendors. He said he would make his people available to help the current contractor find ways to reduce costs. A series of joint breakthrough projects to reorganize the way the contractor carried out maintenance achieved the needed cost reductions without sacrificing ATM availability.

Selecting the Best Multiplication Route

How do you decide which multiplication route is the best way to go? The answer lies somewhere between expediency and sagacity.

During the early stages of the breakthrough strategy, the most important aim is to establish a pattern of success and a sense of momentum. These can be achieved by applying to the selection of expansion projects the guidelines used in Chapter 5 to select initial projects. Keep focused on the areas of real urgency, where people are willing to commit the time and resources needed to get a job done. Set first-step subgoals. Make sure each step is bottom-line and measurable. Go where the readiness is greatest. Make sure there is success. And fun. And excitement.

In making the transition from the first few breakthroughs into expansion efforts, it is good to reinforce the central theme of the overall goal enunciated at the beginning—such as improvement in quality, or enhanced customer service, or far-reaching reductions in operational costs. Thus, to the extent possible, each breakthrough project should reflect the unified sense of priorities established by the organization. At these early stages, however, it is more important to create momentum than to create neatness. Blasting the organization free from the ironclad grip of its institutionalized barriers is the main task. There will be time enough later for shaping, ordering and refining priorities once momentum is gained.

≫ *Managing the Breakthrough Expansion*

To use the breakthrough strategy as a pathway to significant, dramatic, and sustained performance improvement, in addition to a few immediate improvements, senior management will want to establish a number of mechanisms during the initial phases that can be used later to support, nurture, and drive widespread multiplication.

≫ *Managing the Breakthrough Expansion*

1. The Steering Committee
2. Communication With Nonparticipants
3. Workshops to Introduce the Breakthrough Strategy
4. Internal Facilitators

---

1. The Steering Committee

A senior management steering committee can help to orchestrate a major performance improvement effort based on the breakthrough strategy. This group might consist of a regular senior management group—such as a division general manager and his cabinet, a vice president of manufacturing and his direct reports, or a sales director and the key sales support staff and managers. Managers who have an important leadership role to play in a major turnaround should be included even if they hold lower organizational positions. At Metropolitan Community Bank, for example, the steering committee consisted of the managers of ATM installation, service, systems development, and marketing.

The steering committee can help select and launch the early breakthrough projects. It can make sure that people understand the relationship between the individual projects and the overall goals of the organization. The steering committee can decide who should be held accountable for each project and can see to it that appropriate assignments are issued to the managers. It can review progress and help gain support for the projects. And it can take the lead in creating the framework for a longer term improvement process.

2. Communication With Nonparticipants

One of the roles a steering committee can perform is generating plenty of publicity about breakthrough successes. Inviting other managers and employees to progress reviews of the breakthrough projects is one communication mechanism.

Company newspapers can also be used to spread the word. In Pennwalt's Calvert City plant, the plant newspaper had frequent, detailed articles about the progress on reducing hydrofluoric acid costs. In Motorola's Mobile Division, consultants who had helped launch breakthrough projects to speed the introduction of three new radios interviewed a number of participants and then wrote a report on "key learnings." The report was circulated widely within the division and in other Motorola units. The division also had "town meetings" in which the work on accelerating new product development was described to the entire work force.

3. Workshops to Introduce the Breakthrough Strategy

To launch performance improvement projects with a number of managers at once, it is useful to bring them together to learn how to run a breakthrough project. These orientation meetings are work sessions as well as learning sessions because the managers who participate identify initial projects and plan how to get them going quickly after the workshop.

Gus Adack, the executive vice president of the Federal Reserve Bank in Philadelphia, was concerned about his bank's eleventh-place cost ranking in the twelve-bank Federal Reserve system. "I could reduce costs tomorrow by consolidating departments and laying people off," he said, "but my people wouldn't learn anything that way. We need a core of sophisticated managers who can manage ongoing improvement."

Managers from Accounting, Systems, Fiscal Operations, Maintenance, and the bank's other departments met in workshops designed to crystallize an improvement strategy, set specific goals, and develop project work plans. After the workshops, the managers moved into action on projects such as improving space utilization, cutting building heat losses, and reducing the amount and cost of paperwork. Each project focused on a specific cost reduction goal. The improvement efforts then expanded to operating departments such as Check Processing, Financial Services, and Marketing. The combined impact of cost reductions and volume gains pushed Philadelphia to a fourth-place ranking in the Federal Reserve performance evaluation done nine months later. Chapter 10 will describe in more detail how workshops can be used to launch a results-focused management development process.

4. Internal Facilitators

Many managers who read about the breakthrough strategy or hear about it at a management meeting are able to translate the ideas into action on their own. Sometimes the application of just a few key ideas is enough to help them accomplish their goals. But organizations using the breakthrough strategy to make very fundamental or far-reaching improvements can usually benefit from the assistance of facilitators playing a catalytic role in the process. Outside consultants can help launch the approach. To sustain and expand it throughout an organization, however, internal people must play the facilitator's role.

Some of the facilitators' functions are:

> ❯ Presenting workshops: An internal facilitator can help groups of managers learn not only the breakthrough methodology but how to organize performance improvement efforts in their own areas.
>
> ❯ Supporting breakthrough projects: The facilitator can act as a consultant to managers who are organizing and launching projects. The facilitator can run mini-workshops with project teams and can provide backup consultation to managers who are leading the projects.

As a consultant to senior management, the facilitator can sit on the steering committee to help work out an overall performance improvement strategy that links breakthroughs to strategic change.

> Sharing information: The internal facilitator can take responsibility for disseminating information, visiting other companies to find out what they have accomplished, and bringing early successes within the organization to the attention of others to spark their interest in taking a first improvement step.

> Documenting: The internal facilitator can keep a record of the change process within the company, and then circulate pertinent documentation to others in the organization. As the process expands, the documentation makes it possible to involve larger numbers of managers. In some companies, manuals have been prepared to describe how the breakthrough strategy has been used. Model forms help managers prepare project assignments, work plans, temporary organization arrangements, and so forth.

Who should the internal facilitators be? Each company needs to decide this according to its own circumstances. In some companies, the role is seen as a vehicle for putting training specialists to work on the most critical issues the company faces. At PPG Industries a marketing manager took on the facilitator role because creating a new, more central role for the marketing function was a pivotal issue. Where quality has been the central focus of an improvement process, quality control people have been facilitators.

The European manager of an American chemical company decided that he himself could do the best job of getting the message across and teaching the methodology. He conducted breakthrough workshops with key managers in every country where the company had a branch. He was able to use the process not only in setting goals and in organizing the work, but in helping his managers learn how to step up to the more strenuous demands he was placing on them.

» *A Structure For Broad-Scale Progress*

In this chapter, we've considered several ways to multiply breakthrough successes, and we've discussed ways of managing this expansion. Let's see how this is all put together.

In Chapter 1, we saw how the Amstar Corporation began to confront adverse market conditions by achieving a success on one small sugar packaging line. Since that project in 1982, Amstar has been using just about every one of the multiplication mechanisms.

Amstar Continues the Expansion

Amstar's Baltimore refinery gained a foothold on improvement by reducing bag breakage and overfilling on one line within six weeks.

When it appeared that the first project was succeeding, Ron Frey, the employee relations manager, began to work with refinery manager Frank Stowe and production manager Bill Stewart to plan the next steps. They continued to focus on waste reduction—this time on a 5-pound bag packaging line that ran on all three shifts. This line was more highly automated than the first line had been, and so several packaging mechanics were added to the breakthrough project team. Frey designated one of his staff to serve as facilitator on this project and on the ones that would follow. This second project yielded results that were as substantial as those of the first and widened the circle of people and functions exposed to the breakthrough concepts.

Stowe then expanded into other refinery departments. He began several projects in the maintenance department, where they gradually reduced costly downtime on the crane used to unload sugar from ships by 50 percent. Next, significant reductions in material usage were achieved throughout the refinery.

Step by step, additional projects were launched. Within a year and a half, every department had generated substantial savings, with essentially the same people and equipment that had been there all along. Frank Stowe established the Productivity Improvement Steering Committee, consisting of the top refinery managers, to review progress regularly, identify new opportunities, and make improvement a never-ending process.

Replication: All Beginnings Are New

In the summer of 1984, Frank Stowe told the Baltimore story in a speech to a group of Amstar executives. Armando Abay, manager of the Chalmette refinery located near New Orleans, was impressed and decided to test the breakthrough strategy at his plant.

There had been little history of collaboration between management and union at the Chalmette refinery. Readiness for change at the Chalmette refinery was a key roadblock and would have to be built starting with small steps.

To begin the process, Abay, his employee relations manager, Rob Shelton, and production manager, Ken Zimko, chose to involve a small group of supervisors and hourly workers to improve production and filling accuracy on one packaging line. According to Shelton, the project began amid a great deal of skepticism. "When the project leader was told of his responsibilities, he couldn't have been less enthusiastic. And the rest felt the same way."

With acceptance by union officials, the model of Baltimore was used in Chalmette. In October 1984, the project team met to set an eight-week breakthrough goal on the confectioners' sugar packaging line. The team identified five causes of bagging machine downtime—such as mechanical breakdowns, problems with the raw material supply, sticking scales, and slow changeovers from one product to another—and they experimented with solutions. By the end of November, they had achieved a 34 percent increase in 25-pound bag production and a 22 percent increase in 50-pound bag production. During this time, attitudes about the process began to shift. Shelton explained, "At first no one really wanted to own the project—that is, until we started getting results. Then everyone got excited and wanted to be associated with the success."

Unfortunately, a strike broke the momentum. Weeks later, when the work force returned, Abay was worried that the still tense relations between hourly workers and supervisors might undermine the performance of a new breakthrough team. He decided to allow some cooling-off time, and he renewed the breakthrough work by organizing a team made up entirely of salaried personnel. A team of supervisors established the initial goal—to reduce the time for loading outgoing packaged product trucks. They conducted brainstorming sessions, created work plans, and issued assignments. This was an exciting time for those project participants as they saw what could be accomplished through this process. Some weeks later, the manager of the shipping department brought his hourly people together. He described the breakthrough goal and asked if they had any improvement ideas. He was staggered by the number of suggestions they contributed. Obviously, these were ideas that the hourly workers had thought of long before, but had kept to themselves. Commenting on the meeting, the shipping manager said, "I'm sure those people went home that night and told their families that they had been asked their opinion for the first time."

Migrating from Bags to Molasses

Back at Baltimore, one internal facilitator had been designated to provide assistance to the teams. At Chalmette, Rob Shelton decided the process would move faster with a different approach. His idea was to build a core of supervisors and engineers skilled in conducting breakthrough projects. Shelton and an outside consultant designed and led a workshop for breakthrough project leaders. To ensure that the workshop would not be just another stimulating but quickly forgotton training session, the participants actually defined the projects they would launch, after the workshop, in the refining, packaging, shipping, and maintenance departments.

When liquefied, filtered sugar is boiled and the grains of sugar are recrystallized, the sticky, black material left over is called blackstrap molasses. Because they have little market value, the two million gallons of blackstrap produced every year at Chalmette are virtually given away by the refinery. Any sugar left in the solution is given away with the molasses, and that sugar content can approach 50 percent.

A breakthrough team in the refining department set a goal to reduce the sugar content of the blackstrap molasses. The project involved educating the work force on the purpose of the goal, training the equipment operators, making processing changes, and designing improvements in the methods of testing the sugar content of the molasses. As the work yielded substantial savings, the team recognized that their newly developed technical skills and knowledge could be applied earlier in the refining process, when a coating of molasses was removed from the raw sugar. Together, these two projects reduced the sugar content of blackstrap by 3 percent—a small number, but a large cost reduction—which was seen as a step toward even larger gains.

"We'll Run It All With a Bicycle Pump"

Compressed-air usage within the Chalmette refinery had been a problem for a number of years. Two compressors had long supplied the needs of the refinery; but by 1985, the refinery needed four running constantly, at an annual cost of more than $50,000 each. When the question of increased air usage was raised, there were plenty of good "explanations," such as "Production levels are higher. We're doing more maintenance. Of course we're using more air!" But a careful listener could hear the hiss of air escaping through leaks in the pipes and hoses running throughout the refinery.

A team from the maintenance and repair department set a breakthrough goal of bringing air usage down to three compressors. They decided to focus first in one area of refining, the washhouse. In a brainstorming session, which included processing-equipment mechanics and operators, there was an outpouring of enthusiasm and support. Participants asserted that in the past they had often reported air leaks to Maintenance. But Maintenance, overloaded with requests more directly related to daily output, rarely responded, and the workers had gradually stopped reporting the leaks.

Now a team with a goal and a deadline had the authority to get the leaks fixed. People identified leaking pipes and hoses and also pointed out inappropriate uses of compressed air in the washhouse. Mechanics were assigned responsibility for making the repairs. Within two weeks, the team reduced air usage from four compressors to three. The managers running the project began to ask what kinds of additional savings could be made. Someone joked, "We'll run the whole refinery on one bicycle pump."

As the compressed-air team prepared to move to other areas in the refinery, Ken Zimko from the production area came to talk to the project manager. "I was walking through my department last Sunday," said Zimko, "when none of the packaging machines were operating, and I could hear air leaking everywhere! I'd like to send a representative to your meeting to find out how you're getting results." The representative from Production attended the meeting and listened as the team made reports and issued assignments for the next breakthrough steps in the refining department. A team was then established in the production department, and three weeks later the refinery's air usage was down to two compressors. Putting up with the boasting of the original team members seemed a reasonable price to pay for annual savings of more than $100,000. Plans were developed to make sure there would be no backslipping.

Breakthroughs Are Linked to Planning

With breakthroughs moving ahead in all departments in Chalmette and, as had occurred in Baltimore, the fundamental culture of the refinery gradually shifting to a more results-focused, collaborative approach, Armando Abay took the expansion one step further. In a meeting with his department heads, he informed them that the breakthrough strategy would become part of their yearly planning process. In their annual plans, each of them was to identify at least two major breakthrough projects and connect them to the accomplishment of key goals. By 1987, the link between longer term planning and short-term performance improvement was beginning to be forged at Chalmette.

❯❯ *A Cycle of Success Replaces a Cycle of Frustration*

The Amstar experience illustrates the tremendous gains that can be made through persevering application of the breakthrough strategy. Consider what happens as the process expands.

Gradually, goals that previously had been too large, too complex, and apparently unattainable with the resources available, that were seen as the responsibility of "the other person," are divided up and successfully attacked one at a time. Managers learn how to get moving toward immediate results and how to use the experience gained during first projects as the basis for moving forward to additional gains. There's no one waiting around anymore for studies to be carried out and programs to be installed.

Managers begin to focus on what can be accomplished right away—not on how they can get more resources, more help, better equipment, better systems, or better information. They focus their energies on sharply defined, specific, bottom-line goals. They begin to differentiate activity that is directly aimed toward such goals from activity that is not.

Initial successes reveal to managers that they have not been exploiting what they already have. They learn to appreciate what their people are ready, willing, and able to do—rather than focus on employee resistance or incompetence.

Managers become more skilled at making demands and establishing expectations. There is no area where the payback is faster than in the area of demand-making. Once managers realize how important it is to be absolutely clear with a subordinate about the "contract for improvement," they become much less casual about how they discuss goals. They don't feel defeated so easily when subordinates raise doubts about whether higher goals are attainable. They listen to the reservations more carefully, but "hang in there" with their expectations more resolutely—not arbitrarily, not unkindly, but with a new level of perseverance. Standards of acceptable performance steadily increase.

The idea of individual accountability for results takes root. It becomes accepted that there must be one manager who makes each breakthrough goal his or her's to achieve. And that manager has to recruit, deploy, and coordinate the necessary resources to get the job done. They learn that accountability means accomplishing the result— not just giving it a good try.

The use of work planning disciplines increases. People become more comfortable with the need to put assignments of responsibility in writing, to carefully outline and publish work plans, and to hold disciplined progress reviews regularly.

Hierarchical and functional walls begin to erode. As managers take personal responsibility for results, they feel increasingly free to reach down, up, and across to involve people in achieving results. And they discover the willingness and ability of others to provide that help.

Managers learn to set up temporary structures—interlocking systems of work groups—to get projects accomplished. They also learn when to disband those units. Major changes are less of a crisis in the life of the organization. Breakthrough projects help managers learn to make constant change and improvement part of their routine.

And amazingly, time is found to get it all done. Managers learn to organize and control results-producing activity without decreasing efficiency. They find out how to run faster meetings. They can juggle more projects at once. The work planning disciplines become more a way of life. No longer do managers feel torn between immediate tasks and longer range goals; instead, they learn how to link the two into a single chain of activities.

New Cultural Patterns Evolve

All of these elements, acting together, create a shift of attitudes, habit patterns, disciplines, working relationships, policies, and procedures. In short, the basic culture of the organization begins to shift. And it shifts in profound and permanent ways.

There is a startling contrast to the experience of companies that have wasted untold millions of dollars in efforts to "shift their culture"—through training programs, inspirational efforts, slogans, and presidential speeches, all in the vain hope that once they manage to change the culture, the company's performance would spurt upwards.

The logic must be stood on its head: cultures are changed when the things that happen day by day, at every level within the company, begin to change. Rarely with a big splash, hundreds of reinforcing changes in how tasks are accomplished and goals achieved create fundamental shifts in the overall work patterns of the organization. Without addressing "the need to change the culture," the breakthrough strategy accomplishes that very aim.

>> PART III

Breakthrough Projects: Vehicles for Innovation

8

>> From Proselytizers to Allies: A Shifting Role for Staff Specialists

The fact that American business is losing ground competitively can never be blamed on the lack of expert help. Repeated studies have shown that in most companies, the population of support staff, technicians, and internal consultants is astronomically higher in America than in other parts of the world. All these staff people are bolstered by uncounted thousands of consultants outside the companies.

Yet countries with many fewer experts are accomplishing much more; it is clear that this huge national powerhouse of technical and professional capability is failing, by a wide margin, to make the impact it could be making. This great, misused reserve of expertise is important not only for whatever direct contributions it makes but because these experts are also the innovators who design the systems, processes, methods, and technologies that affect the efficiency of everyone else's work.

The fault does not lie in their innovations, which are, for the most part, technically sound. Success, however, depends on the ability and willingness of operating managers to use innovations. In earlier chapters, we saw that when technical and organizational innovations are introduced with the assumption that they will work their magic and bring about significant improvements, the results are frequently disappointing. Unless deliberate steps are taken to avoid it, the organization's built-in barriers almost inevitably undermine the benefits of the innovations.

Results-focused breakthrough projects, by contrast, permit managers to break free of the inhibitions imposed by the barriers. The clear-cut accountability for results, sense of urgency, short time span, and experimental nature of these projects make them ideal vehicles for the successful introduction of new systems, methods, and procedures. Senior managers and staff experts can take advantage of this natural context for innovation.

>> The Challenge for the Staff Specialist

In workshops with many hundreds of staff specialists whose mission is to introduce innovative technologies, I have asked them to assess the impact of their efforts. On the technical side, these staff specialists introduce automation, new computer systems, materials management and inventory control systems, computer-aided manufacturing methods, statistical quality control, strategic planning, and dozens of other engineering and "hard science" techniques. On the organizational and human-resource side, they are the professionals advocating new management techniques, organization structure designs, training and education, employee involvement methods, and reward and incentive systems.

These missionaries of sophisticated management, despite their diverse backgrounds, all share one universal frustration: they are convinced that their tools, techniques, and methodologies have the power to help their companies be much more competitive, but lack of receptivity or motivation by their internal clients prevents greater exploitation of these approaches.

> "Managers seem reluctant to give up their comfortable ways, even though they know imports are making deep inroads into the business."

> "We showed them we can make big bucks with this new system—but they keep putting it off."

"There's a real 'not invented here' factor. Their minds
are closed to ideas."

"There is so much politics that the implementation is
moving at a snail's pace."

Is the problem only with the users' "closed minds" and resistance to change, or do the providers share a responsibility for
the disappointing returns from their efforts?

In the 1950s a group of British anthropologists traveled
through New Guinea and produced a film about their journey.
The leader of the expedition described one village where the
hospitality had been particularly warm and generous. The villagers lived in log cabins and, to obtain logs, had to use primitive
stone axes to fell large trees. "We wanted to do something to
show our gratitude to these people. We presented them with
some sharp steel axes to ease their tasks," said the anthropologist.
Instead of making it easier, however, the steel axes were difficult
for the natives to use. "You see," the anthropologist explained,
"the cutting heads of their stone tools were fastened at right
angles to the end of the handles—like farmers' hoes. Steel blades
are fastened parallel. We noticed some animated conversation
among the villagers and, just before we left, with a great show
of relief, they ceremoniously returned the steel axes to us."

Most corporate staff specialists would smile with sympa-
thetic amusement, watching that tender scene on the screen.
Yet the next day, they might well hand over their version of the
steel axe to people in their companies who are wedded comfortably to their own familiar stone axes.

For example, I have seen systems people installing personal
computers on the desks of senior executives, oblivious to the
fact that these executives are anxious because they don't even
understand the symbols on the keyboard. A staff group in a building supply company constructed a mathematical model showing
that the company could save large amounts of money by reducing its seven warehouses to four. The staff group pointed out
that at least 90 percent of the deliveries from four warehouses
would meet the company's traditional twenty-four-hour delivery
deadline, and none would take more than forty-eight hours. But
senior management was aghast. These relative newcomers, none

of whom had ever sold the product, had the temerity to suggest that the company abandon its long-standing twenty-four-hour guarantee! Every systems, methods, or technical innovation intrudes upon and changes traditional patterns of work and relationships. Even when the innovation is needed, anxiety and discomfort over it can provoke various forms of resistance.

In Chapters 2 and 3, we saw how entrenched barriers can defeat the purposes of the soundest, most professionally installed innovation. And that is the problem with treating technology as if it were the key to progress. If the many other changes necessary to the success of the innovation are not carried out, its potential will never be realized. This simple fact is overlooked constantly by experts who develop new programs, new systems, and new technologies that collide headlong with the institutionalized barriers. To call the disappointing outcomes, "resistance to change," is to miss the real issue.

» Staff Specialist as Change Agent

In order to significantly increase receptivity to new technology and the payback on investment in innovation, staff specialists must shift from being simply purveyors of specialized know-how to becoming effective "change agents" as well.

This is not just a theoretical shift. The staff innovator not only must be knowledgeable within his or her particular field of expertise, but also must be practically skilled in all aspects of translating technical innovations into better business results. In short, the effective staff innovator must become more skilled in helping user managers multiply output: that is, in showing managers how to make better use of resources and how to integrate new sophisticated methods and technologies while doing everything else essential to success.

Staff innovators can make this shift by working along five key lines of progress:

1. Make sure there is early reinforcing success for the users.
2. Design innovations to match user readiness (instead of pitting innovation against user resistance).

3. Share a sense of ownership with the users through collaboration and training.
4. Make sure that senior management makes its demands directly on the user.
5. Break large-scale, long-term projects down into incremental breakthrough goals.

Let's see how staff specialists can use these principles to expand their role in the success of their organizations.

1. Make Sure There Is Early Reinforcing Success for Users

There is always some anxiety on the part of users about the introduction of new technology. Therefore, anything that demonstrates quickly how the innovation can help the user will increase the user's openness to the new technology.

When I made this suggestion some years ago at a conference of systems professionals from General Electric, I was challenged by one participant: "That is a good theory, but you have to understand that a systems project takes six months to a year, or longer. There is no way to have an immediate impact." Before I could respond, another audience member jumped up to tell his story. He had been called in to improve the raw material inventory system for one General Electric plant that had too much inventory overall, but nevertheless experienced frequent stock-outs. One source of the problem was the fact that many containers were not clearly identified and receipt records and labels were incomplete.

Every systems professional would have dealt with this problem as one element of their overall project. But this expert drafted a letter addressed to all suppliers, for the signature of the plant purchasing manager. It declared that suppliers who wanted to remain on the approved vendor list should return a signed copy of the letter agreeing to place certain specified information on the outside label of every shipment sent to the plant. By this one stroke, he enabled the plant to make an immediate gain in its ability to track material and reduce raw material inventory.

The challenger asked, "And how long did that take?" The response: "Three days."

Not everyone can be so fortunate as to have a success in three days, but every staff expert can plan technical changes so as to contribute to short-term performance improvement. This makes the users winners and helps them become comfortable with the new technology.

2. Design Innovations to Match User Readiness

No matter who initiates a project—the line manager or the staff innovator—each will see the needs in his or her own terms. The "objective" facts revealed by the expert's analysis may suggest one approach to a project. But equally important is consideration for what the managers and employees of the particular business are ready, willing, and able to undertake at that moment.

The importance of readiness was illustrated at American Can Company when it still made cans and was not yet Primerica. The managers of one division followed a human-resource specialist's suggestion that they launch an employee involvement campaign in a recently acquired machine tool company named HIMCO. They announced to employees that a large capital investment was about to be made in new space and equipment and that the employees were going to be "partners" in making the shift into more sophisticated production methods. As a first step, management was going to remove all time clocks and pay everyone a salary rather than an hourly wage.

Employees alleged that the move was just an attempt to discourage unionization. Besides, they preferred that their commitment to the company be clearly defined by the hourly wage. That way, when they took off a few hours on an afternoon to go hunting, they could sacrifice the pay but not feel guilty about leaving.

HIMCO's new managers realized that they had tried to take too big a step at once, so they reinstated the hourly wage. Then they assigned to Industrial Engineering and Human Resources the task of selecting a breakthrough project that took into account the readiness of the work force. At the time, plant management was trying to hire a large number of skilled machinists. They had put employment ads in the local newspapers, but had received little response. When the project group asked people why, a few machinists pointed out that HIMCO had always been known as a tough place to work. "You've got to let people know that there's new ownership, and that things will be different now," they advised. "We can help you do that."

Seizing on this readiness to participate, the staff people suggested that top management form a team consisting of managers, supervisors, and workers. This team identified the key selling points of the "new" HIMCO and wrote a new employment ad. When the company was flooded with applications in response to the ad, the next step was taken. As applicants arrived, their skills were screened by the machinists themselves, who had a great interest in determining who their fellow workers would be. And when someone was hired, the people on the shop floor coordinated the new employee's orientation and training.

With this degree of employee involvement established, the staff people advised management to launch a few breakthrough projects focused on goals such as increased recycling of scrap metal and reduction in lost tools. Over the course of several months, step by step, the company established genuine employee involvement. Eventually, employees helped to lay out the new shop and to integrate the new sophisticated machining equipment.

3. Share a Sense of Ownership With the Users

If innovation is seen as the responsibility of staff experts, line managers will never have the same sense of responsibility toward it as they do toward their own goals. Moreover, user managers are busy and are often quite willing to duck out of involvement in new "extra" projects. It is very tempting for competent staff specialists simply to roll up their sleeves and move ahead on their own. Thus, as the work moves forward, the experts become increasingly committed to the outcomes that they have decided are best. The user managers, not having shared in the evolutionary thinking process that led to the conclusions, can be hostile or indifferent to the results, divided among themselves, and worried about whether they can be successful with the new tools.

That is exactly what was happening at our frequently mentioned Bonaventure Terminal. For years, a team of industrial engineers had tried to stimulate improvement in the terminal.

But because they were forever publishing reports that made management seem incompetent, they were regarded as a thorn in everyone's side.

When the terminal's managers launched the initial breakthrough projects, I suggested that they use the industrial engineers to help. "You have to be kidding," said Emmett McGurk, the terminal manager. "They'll just turn the wine to vinegar." With a bit of urging, he agreed to "allow" the engineers to assist with a few technical details. For the engineers, it was a refreshing change: they were now working with managers who wanted to make things happen and were asking for help, not fighting it. Gradually, the very changes the engineers had been promoting were adopted as part of the project. It was a new experience for the managers: they were in charge of the improvements and would get credit for success. The engineers were there just to provide expert help.

4. Make Sure That Senior Management Makes Its Demands Directly on the User

Senior managers who are impatient for improvement, but who lack experience, skill, or confidence in demand-making, often ask staff experts to serve as the engine to drive improvements. When the experts try to get started, however, they discover that the senior manager hasn't made it clear to his subordinates that they must achieve those improvements. When such demands have not been made, the staff expert may become a missionary— trying to persuade the users to accept the help they haven't yet realized they need.

For example, before Bell Canada launched its major turnaround effort, referred to earlier, corporate staff engineers periodically did a thorough "operations review" of every switching center. Everything that needed improvement was carefully detailed in lengthy reports, which were submitted to higher management. The switching center managers, under little pressure to improve operations, perceived the reports as detailed catalogues of their failures and reacted by defending themselves and attacking the reports.

Once the company's performance improvement process was launched, however, every switching center was given very specific cost and service improvement targets. It was made clear that these targets had to be reached; explanations would not be an adequate substitute for actual results. Now, instead of the engineers trying to whip up enthusiasm by center managers who seemed to be resistant or indifferent, the engineers became resources who could help managers under strong pressure figure out how to achieve their goals.

❯❯ Demands Misdirected to Staff

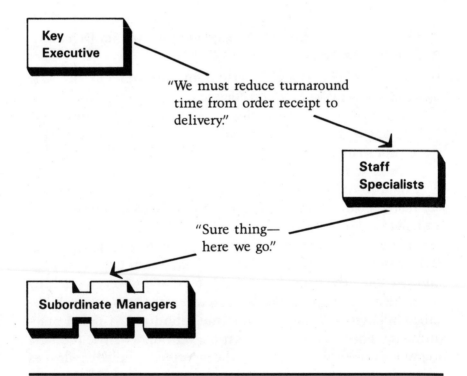

Key Executive

"We must reduce turnaround time from order receipt to delivery."

Staff Specialists

"Sure thing— here we go."

Subordinate Managers

» *Demands Directed to Accountable Managers*

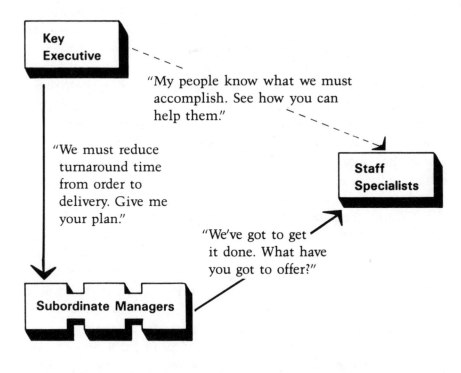

Key
Executive

"My people know what we must accomplish. See how you can help them."

"We must reduce turnaround time from order to delivery. Give me your plan."

Staff
Specialists

"We've got to get it done. What have you got to offer?"

Subordinate Managers

A similar shift occurred at a production facility of American Cyanamid that was experiencing wide fluctuations in the yields of a particular chemical. Experts from corporate headquarters were sent to the plant to uncover the sources of the fluctuations. The implicit message to the plant's managers was: the experts have arrived, and they'll solve the problems.

Despite the best efforts of the experts, however, there was little progress until top management told the plant operations managers in no uncertain terms to get the yields up and keep them there. With the full weight of responsibility on them, the operating managers were happy to enlist the support of the experts, and together, they solved the problem.

5. Break Projects Down into Incremental Goals

If staff experts are to achieve the gains we have been describing, they will have to make one more major adjustment: giving up their fixation with the "all or nothing" or "total systems" approach to innovation. Often, managers who are impatient to accelerate improvement readily embrace innovators who promise that their particular technology or system will provide the key to success. Those managers put all the company's chips on one big bet. For instance, a new organization configuration that could easily be tested first in one or two places is implemented instead across a whole corporation. A quality improvement program that is only a gleam in someone's eye suddenly becomes the touchstone, and every employee is sent for training before the first results are realized.

The systems department at Petro Canada had carefully constructed a comprehensive plan for integrating all the computer functions of the company into one large system. As part of this plan they set to work adapting a general ledger system to fit their integration plans. It was a big job and required the constant involvement of the future users.

This systems department had always taken the view that quality performance meant delivering only fully operational systems. As the project stretched out over two years, at a cost of over $1 million, the users became frustrated and eventually refused to participate. They had stopped believing they would ever benefit from all of this work. The developers kept pushing ahead, pursuing the goal of installing a completed product.

Since the users' involvement was essential, work on the integration plan finally came to a halt. At the suggestion of an outside consultant, one small piece of the general ledger system was selected for immediate development. It would provide some reports that the accountants urgently needed, so they agreed to participate. The systems people set aside their insistence on delivering all or nothing. The project was successful. From that point forward, the project advanced step by step, achieving considerable success—and a warming relationship between systems and users.

Architecture of Incremental Progress

The total systems approach to innovation has a certain compelling logic. Why do it a piece at a time once you've become convinced that this approach will work miracles? Then there is the "economy of scale"—as long as the staff experts are introducing a program or system, why not go all the way at once?

But these large-scale introductions of new technology or new methods are counterproductive to the goal of having individual managers develop a sense of ownership. These managers have trouble getting involved and can play no meaningful role when the project gets too big and too complex. Instead of quick successes, the time frame is stretched out and the payoffs fade very far into the future. It becomes just another staff expert project.

What is needed is breaking projects down into steps, each one of which meets an immediate user need, but also represents progress toward the more comprehensive system. It is easy to overlook the fact that what might appear to the staff expert as just one step in the overall project could, by itself, be a beneficial subproject for the user.

Here are some ways that staff experts can assist in turning small parts of an overall systems project into incremental breakthroughs:

1. *Define the current information flow.* Just helping the user to clarify the nature of the information used for decisions could be a useful contribution—especially if some critical questions are raised about how that information is being used now and how it will be used.

2. *Make the current system work better while waiting for the new system.* As a technical specialist works with line management to define future needs, they can be developing a better understanding of what is going on today. Immediate improvements are often possible—improvements that will not only aid current business operations but also create a stronger base upon which to introduce the new systems.

3. *Improve collaboration among user departments.* Sometimes a systems project can be used to bring various user groups together; the systems staff person

often has unique perspective on the flow of information and decisionmaking. Helping users improve their working methods can be quite useful to them.

4. *Develop one urgently needed element of the overall system.* This is what was done at Petro Canada, where the systems group focused on reports that the accountants were eager to have.

❯❯ *New Role for Staff Specialists and Internal Consultants*

Unless the staff innovator makes a number of interrelated supporting changes simultaneously, his or her sophisticated implant simply will not take hold and accomplish its purpose—any more than a graft that is rejected by a body's immune system.

❯❯ *A Changing Role for Staff Experts*

Begin With Results: The "Breakthrough Approach"	*Instead of:* Beginning With Programs and Preparations
❯ Start *with* Urgent Goals	*instead of with* Problems and Shortcomings
❯ Focus *on* Short-Term Results	*instead of on* Installing Programs, Systems, Training, Technology
❯ Leadership *by* Accountable Manager	*instead of by* Staff Expert
❯ Technical and Systems Innovations Installed **Gradually** to **Support** Progress	*instead of* Installed **All at Once** as the **Key** to Progress

---

Using short-term, focused breakthrough projects as the vehicles for a gradual adaptation to new approaches makes it more likely that (1) the increment of technology will be successful and reward the user, (2) the technology will be integrated into the life of the organization, and (3) the initial successes will become the foundation for an expanding utilization of the new approach.

Staff experts and users must collaborate closely to succeed. This will create a basis for continued collaboration around increasingly sophisticated applications. As managers succeed in using new technology, new systems, or new methods to accomplish results, their confidence increases, their understanding of the methodology improves, and their trust in the experts deepens. Similarly, as professionally trained experts work more collaboratively with managers and have increasing success, their skills in responding to user needs, producing user successes, and incrementally introducing their innovations, are sharpened. Each project is a learning experience for both the technical expert and the user manager.

The next few chapters extend this incremental, results-focused approach for introducing innovations to strategic planning, management development, and quality improvement.

9

>> Tactics for Mastering Strategy

When Bill Stanley returned to his division from the corporation's annual long-range planning meeting, he was feeling quite good. Not only his immediate boss but also some of the other senior executives, and even the heads of other units, had complimented him on the imaginative approach of his division's long-range plan. It recommended selling off one part of the division's business and then—through developing a new family of products and acquiring one or two small companies—breaking into an expanding market that matched the mission of the division. He realized that significant changes would have to be made in organization structure, in new product development, in manufacturing technology, and in countless other areas if he was to realize his very ambitious strategic goals. Bill returned home enthusiastic and eager to get moving as quickly as possible.

When he walked into his office the first morning back, there was a pile of correspondence to be read and the usual "pink slips" for return telephone calls. He had barely begun to dig into these when his sales vice president stopped in to give him some bad news. It appeared that second-quarter sales would fall short of budget by more than 15 percent. And at that late date, there was no way to prevent inventory and other related costs from going over budget.

Bill could not avoid dealing with these issues. Corporate management's warm feelings about his strategic plans would chill within minutes after bad news like this hit headquarters. He asked his secretary to invite his key people to join him in the conference room after lunch. There they worked until 10:00 p.m. on how to respond to the problem.

And so it went in the weeks and months that followed. Although he talked a few times with his personnel director about hiring a person to search for acquisitions, very little of Bill's time was devoted to the strategic plan and its implementation. Each day brought a fresh supply of immediate challenges, problems, and crises that had to be dealt with.

What's the matter? Here is a manager determined to do what good managers are supposed to be doing—gaining market share and beating the competition by identifying and making the right strategic moves. But Bill Stanley is caught in a dilemma: in the race against tough domestic and worldwide competition, he has been taught that strategic change is the key to ultimate success; yet he's trapped in day-to-day preoccupations.

Stanley is not exceptional. The great majority of managers are fighting this same battle. Moreover, many of them are feeling guilty or incompetent because they believe they should be able to escape from their day-to-day preoccupations and concentrate on long-term strategy. That is one of the most commonly accepted—and destructive—ideas about what managers should be doing to upgrade their companies' capacity to compete.

›› Strategic Planning: An Escape from Gravity?

An article by Wickham Skinner, in the July–August 1986 issue of the *Harvard Business Review*, "The Productivity Paradox," illustrates how American managers have been browbeaten into accepting this view of themselves. Skinner dismisses most short-term efforts to improve performance, asserting that "by tying managers at all levels to short-term considerations, [the typical productivity programs] short circuit the development of an aggressive manufacturing strategy." He outlines many of the shortcomings that have affected productivity and performance improvement efforts and then asserts, in effect, that the only sound alternative is to shift attention and concentrate on strategic manufacturing issues, such as long-term capacity planning, plant sizes and locations, make versus buy decisions, and so forth.

Of course, these important strategic issues must be dealt with. But in this article—which was awarded the *Review's* McKinsey Prize for 1986—Skinner asserts that managers are really wasting their time when they become preoccupied with short-term improvements. Skinner has plenty of company. Most of us are familiar with Peter Drucker's observation, "It is more important to do the right things than to do things right." Many other critics assert that managers must make this choice: give up the focus on performance and concentrate on strategy. This advice can be dangerous for those who actually try to follow it, and depressing for those who realize that it cannot safely be followed. Professor Drucker's dictum notwithstanding, the ability to do the right things is almost always inextricably linked to the ability to do things right.

Strategic thinking, probing and investigation require time and energy. Only self-confident managers with time to think and freedom from constant crises can visualize creative scenarios. Unless managers know that the day-to-day job is under control and the necessary improvements are being made, they will not have the time, the perspective, the self-confidence, or the good working relationships that are all essential to imaginative strategic thinking and decisionmaking.

And even if managers were able to put aside their preoccupation with next month's results, on what basis would they be able to assess what their organization ought to accomplish in the next few years? If they base their projections on their company's current performance, they might take too limited a view of what's possible. For example, at the Pennwalt Calvert City plant whose hydrofluoric acid costs were out of line, the "prudent" strategic decision might have been to get out of the business.

For the organization that has not learned how to break out of its self-constraints, strategic planning may be too limited an exercise.

Worse, managers in such companies, frustrated by the limitations of past performance, may have Superman fantasies of leaping over tall buildings in a single bound. Mao Tse-tung did this in the 1960s with an entire country, when he tried to make China a modern steel-producing nation by creating thousands of "backyard blast furnaces." The resources wasted and the time lost by this effort have never been fully assessed. Managers fall into the same trap when they develop strategy without linking it to a realistic view of what their organizations can achieve.

By the Way, Plans Require Execution

Even supposing that managers could put aside their concerns about inventory, cash management, delivery schedules, productivity, monthly sales quotas, and other short-term issues and concentrate on creating ambitious strategic goals, what would happen when they went to translate their strategic ideas into effective change? They'd find that execution can be the soft underbelly of strategy. How long has Detroit known that it would be strategically wise to make a safe, stylish, high-quality small car? When did U.S. consumer electronics companies realize that there would be a huge market for VCRs? Without the capacity to execute well, the best-conceived strategies may become mere illusions that fade as implementation plans falter, as attention is drawn off to cope with shortfalls in current results, or as the better executors—even starting later—move in and deliver a better product, cheaper and faster.

For example, twenty years ago, a few senior managers of the *New York Times* recognized that their worldwide news-gathering network, unique in the industry, was an underexploited asset. All those resources were going into the production of a newspaper for a single market. Why not set up regional editions of the *Times*—as the *Wall Street Journal* had begun to do? Andrew Fisher, then the executive vice president, took the lead, and a western edition was launched. In those days, the *Times*—as has been well reported in a number of books—consisted of a number of fiefdoms headed by managers who jealously guarded their own prerogatives and were not really interested in collaboration or change. The ingredients did not exist for the success of any new venture that required interfunctional cooperation and the sharing of credit. Strategically, the idea of a regional edition was brilliant; nevertheless, after a brief existence, the western edition was quietly buried.

In the intervening years, Publisher Arthur O. Sulzberger and President Walter Mattson recruited and promoted a "new breed" of executives and aggressively pursued innovative business strategies. The *New York Times* developed capacities that it did not have when it launched the western edition. Recently, the company resurrected the idea of regional editions and now publishes in a number of locations around the country—illustrating that the value of a strategy depends on the present capacity of an organization to make it succeed.

» *Accelerating the Move to Strategic Planning*

Managers should stop berating themselves for their tactical preoccupations. There is no way that they can ignore the demands of current performance. There are too many pressures built into our economic system that require them to pay attention to those demands. Stockholders want returns. Banks want to be paid. Top management's success is measured by quarterly results as well as by strategic thrusts. Those short-term pressures are all-demanding and will defeat any attempt to avoid them. The solution lies in accomplishing short-term goals in ways that simultaneously strengthen the company's capacity to effect strategic changes. Organizations do not have to wait ten or twenty years until the conditions for successful strategic thrusts evolve. Management can rapidly accelerate the process.

Some years ago, I was asked to help a community hospital in New England create a ten-year plan. When I arrived on the scene, I discovered an appallingly low level of communication among the hospital's trustees, administration, and medical staff. There was little chance that those factions could work together to create a sound, coherent, long-range view of the hospital.

Moreover, if a plan were to be created without the participation of all three groups, it would be merely a piece of fiction. Such a plan would never have been accepted and carried out. The first thing to do was to get the groups working together successfully in some new ways.

Where to begin was not difficult to determine. Some months before, the mayor's nephew had been brought into the emergency room after an accident and, through some oversight, had been kept waiting over an hour before a physician saw him. That made headlines in the local newspaper. The article used the incident to highlight the "poor service" being provided by the hospital, with special scrutiny given to the emergency and radiology facilities.

Two teams were assembled—each consisting of some physicians, some trustees, and some administrators. One aimed at improving how patients were received and cared for in radiology; the other focused on treatment in the emergency room.

These two task teams provided an opportunity for the hospital's factions to collaborate to attack joint goals. And they were successful. A few other task groups were soon established. Gradually, along with better results came new ways of working together on projects and a better relationship among medical staff, administrative personnel, and trustees. Attacking short-term issues in the right way created the environment needed to take on longer range planning. Within about six months, it was possible to launch a successful study of where the hospital should be headed.

Strategy in a Salt Mine

Mines Seleine was another organization too preoccupied with immediate issues to deal effectively with strategy.

One hundred twenty miles off the coast of Nova Scotia lie the Magdalen Islands. Settled by English and French fishermen, most of the people on these picturesque, windswept islands are employed by two industries—tourism and fishing. On one of the islands there is also a salt mine. Run by Mines Seleine, a corporation owned by the Province of Quebec, this mine under the ocean floor is reached from its entrance on the surface of the island. The salt is brought up through the mine shaft, crushed, purified, and stored on the island until it is shipped to depots in Canada and the United States, where it is used on icy winter roads.

Headquartered in Montreal, the company had been operating in the red since the mine opened. In 1986 the board of directors, intent on establishing profitability, appointed a new president, John Gillman, who was a well-respected mining engineer with many years of experience in the industry. Gillman decided that the first order of business was to identify some future directions for the company, for both the short and long term. Mines Seleine had always done yearly budgetary planning, but it had never really clarified its business strategies and key priorities.

In preparation for a planning session in November 1986, Gillman asked his senior managers in Mine Operations, Transportation and Distribution, Sales, and Administration to answer two questions about the direction of the business: (1) What are the key issues in your area that need to be addressed? and (2) What factors are critical to the success of Mines Seleine in the coming year?

Discussions with his managers and their written answers to these questions suggested to Gillman that the managers felt overwhelmed by the day-to-day "fire fighting" that characterized their jobs: dealing with poor salt quality and the financial penalties imposed because of it; collecting on overdue accounts; handling delays in shipping; making quick pricing decisions; and many other operational details. Recognizing that plans for immediate performance improvement would be the most important result of this first planning session, John Gillman asked each manager to prepare a list of suggested improvement goals for his area over the next year. In addition, to begin the process of looking more to the future, the sales director was asked to prepare a presentation on Mines Seleine's market and competition, while Gillman himself prepared a draft statement of the company's mission, long-term goals, and key business indicators.

At the planning meeting the following month, the group discussed Gillman's draft mission statement and long-term goals. The focus then shifted. One at a time, each functional manager highlighted the factors critical for short-term success in his area—such as salt quality, safety, cost reduction, customer service. The group then helped the functional manager choose his most critical goals. For each goal, a deadline was set and a "godfather"—*parrain* in French—was selected to be responsible for its accomplishment. A consultant helped the managers to refine their goals, create project work plans, and establish a process for regular progress reviews.

A number of breakthrough projects were organized, most of them directed towards immediate cost reduction. For instance:

> ❯ Amending a transportation contract to save $50,000 annually
> ❯ Reducing the time required to recover receivables
> ❯ Eliminating unnecessary spare parts from inventory
> ❯ Completing a new offshore depot to reduce transportation costs

At this initial planning stage, only one breakthrough project of a more strategic nature was identified. Mines Seleine wanted to reduce its dependence on its principal market, the Province of Quebec. The management team decided to work with an agent in the Atlantic Provinces to analyze the market and transportation options there and to determine the locations where cost advantages would allow Mines Seleine to make winning bids.

By June of 1987, only six months later, most of the performance breakthroughs had been accomplished, saving hundreds of thousands of dollars a year. The work in the Atlantic Provinces had resulted in a substantial new market where Mines Seleine had never sold before. The gains moved the company into operating profitability. The process also gave the managers a new sense of mastery over their own destiny, which they could now begin to translate into planning for longer term strategic directions.

Performance Breakthroughs Create Strategic Power

The experiences of the New England hospital and Mines Seleine illustrate that successful breakthrough projects—focused as these were on short-term performance improvements rather than on strategic shifts—can begin to establish the climate, the relationships, and the skills that are essential to effective strategic management. The use of management disciplines is strengthened. So is management's capacity to develop plans and take the steps that get them to where they want to be. So is the idea that one manager can be accountable for a project involving many different groups. All these abilities are essential to effective strategic planning and actions.

Gradually, the hospital extended performance improvement projects to other areas, projects similar to those begun in the emergency room and the radiology department. At the same time, it began to look ahead. A few teams composed, like the performance improvement teams, of trustees, doctors, and administrators began to analyze demographic trends in the community and to review the plans of other hospitals and health-related agencies in the vicinity. This was the beginning of a truly collaborative strategic effort, made possible only by the initial performance-focused breakthrough successes. The outcome was a bold and imaginative vision for the hospital, one much more ambitious than anyone would have dared to suggest earlier.

In the same way, improvements in performance capability and working relationships at Mines Seleine set the stage for important strategic shifts. After their success in opening one Atlantic Province market, they organized some strategic breakthrough projects. Starting with the broad goal, "We need to expand our business further in the Atlantic Provinces," they narrowed down to a few selected communities in Nova Scotia. They won initial contracts in those communities and then began developing the transportation and storage infrastructure necessary for further expansion.

Having brought their company back to profitability and opened up some new markets, and with the confidence created by those successes, the top managers were ready to take a look at new business opportunities. They analyzed how they were transporting their salt. (Transportation has always been the major cost for all bulk commodities.) As a result, they acquired the marine transportation company they had been using. Their next step was to find a way to counterbalance the seasonal nature of their business. They identified and acquired the license to distribute a chemical that mixes with salt to melt ice at even lower temperatures but that also can be used to keep dust down on rural roads during the summer months. Because the chemical is used by the same customers buying its salt, the new product fitted right into Mines Seleine's existing distribution system.

The hospital and the salt mine company show vividly how performance breakthroughs provide the experiences, the skills, and the work disciplines required for strategic planning and create the sense of confidence and mastery that permits managers to make more sophisticated strategic plans and realize them successfully.

» *Strategic Business Breakthroughs*

People with faith in astrology may wait patiently for the proper alignment of planets, stars, and moon before taking certain important steps. Some managers do the same thing with strategy. They create long-range plans, then wait until the "right circumstances" make it possible to act on those plans. This pattern reinforces the tendency to design strategic decisions as cataclysmic, go-for-broke events, since managers are banking on them to yield dramatic changes in the life of the organization. No wonder managers want to wait.

Yet it is almost always possible to carve off a few incremental, low-risk steps, from the big strategic plans. Doing that can open the door to immediate action.

Take the Mobile Division of Motorola, mentioned earlier, as an example. This business, which manufactures two-way radios used in vehicles, recognized that its market was beginning to change. Traditionally, most customers had wanted the highest performance product, for which they were willing to pay the necessary price. But demand was gradually growing for products that were less expensive and offered fewer options. The division began building low-end radios as it continued to supply the most versatile equipment to those who needed it.

As any manufacturing manager knows, however, a company building high-end products—whose benefits to demanding customers outweigh their modest price differentials—and a company producing for the low-end market are run quite differently from each other. Many services essential for the high-end product are unnecessary "frills" for the low-end. Moreover, while high-end products can be sold with individual attention to each customer and each sale, low-end products have to be distributed differently.

Over time it became clear to the division's managers—and to their superiors—that the division should be split into two separate businesses, with separate management structures, separate locations, and probably different distribution channels. The division was housed at that time in a single modern facility in Fort Worth. Considering the number of major changes that would have to be planned and carried out—as well as the individual bailiwicks that would have to be divided up—it looked as though it would take several years of hard work to make this strategic shift.

Group Vice President Mort Topfer declared that they had to move more quickly than that. What could they do at once right there at Fort Worth? In response to that question, they created an answer: without moving a single piece of equipment, they set up "two companies," high-end and low-end, right on the spot. Of course, there were tough decisions that had to be made in accounting for expenses and related issues. But deciding to act instead of getting delayed by studies and preparations, they took a major step toward the strategic goal and, at the same time, were able to test the concept in practice. Today the two divisions are completely separate.

If the same kind of thinking that goes into carving off first steps from large-scale performance objectives is applied to long-term strategic directions, the result is a *strategic* breakthrough project. The first step taken toward splitting the two businesses at the Mobile Division of Motorola is a good example. Such a project starts with a large-scale strategic plan or goal that is still in the "concept" or idea phase and derives from it an achievable breakthrough goal, loaded for success. While all breakthrough projects are aimed at contributing to longer term goals, these strategic breakthrough projects are explicitly designed to help management to:

❯ enter a new market or redefine the market;
❯ change products or product mix;

❭ redefine service;
❭ make shifts in basic technology; and/or
❭ relocate company facilities.

❭❭ *New York Telephone Customer Network Design*

After the AT&T divestiture, the new regional telephone operating companies were quickly faced with small competitors entering particular niches of their markets and beginning to serve customers more rapidly, more effectively, and at lower prices. The operating companies would have to revamp themselves to succeed in this new competitive environment. Central to the "revamping" strategy of the New York Telephone Company were two major thrusts: (1) to get much closer to the customer, and (2) to become the low-cost producer.

When it was part of AT&T, New York Telephone had concentrated on developing the best new communications technology and then offering it to the customer. This technology-driven approach continually expanded the capabilities of telephone systems, but often prevented the company from being able to respond to the unique needs of single customers. Once the market was opened up to competition, however, plenty of companies emerged that were eager to meet the unique needs of every customer out there. New York Telephone had to become much more customer-responsive. But in a company of 50,000 people, such a fundamental change is a monumental challenge.

The engineers in the network planning department designed the sophisticated services needed by large companies, such as data communications, backup networks, and internal telephone networks. These engineers were properly proud of their technical achievements.

Typically, Network Planning would develop a telecommunications product that was then priced by one group, marketed by another, and sold by still another. The sales group responded to requests from potential customers by offering selections from the existing product line. When a one-of-a-kind request came in—such as a request for a network to link sixty-four New York State university campuses, or a request for a unique backup telecommunication system in case of a disaster—sales had no good way to respond. Network Planning, which did have the expertise to design these systems, was rarely brought in on these one-of-a-kind system requests.

A Low-Risk Strategic Experiment

Tom Dillon and Bill McGruther of Network Planning were eager to overcome these traditional obstacles. They were frustrated by the distance between their technical people and the customer, so they decided to try something different. As an experiment, they asked Bill Gibbons, a network services engineer in upstate New York, to go to two of New York Telephone's most important clients in the region, a large bank and a campus of the State University of New York. His mission: find out what they needed, and then see that they got it.

Gibbons and his team of two engineers went directly to the telecommunications managers at the bank and at the campus, asked questions, and identified the major frustrations of these managers. "The bank had heavy communication needs with the financial district in New York City, which were not being met," Gibbons explained.

> They were ready to investigate alternative suppliers if we couldn't solve their problems. And SUNY—the state university—is a large customer with expanding communications requirements. If we couldn't meet the needs of this one campus, we wouldn't be in a good position to retain their overall business in the long run.

Gibbons carefully explained his mission to the New York Telephone marketing and operations people assigned to those two accounts. They were happy to see engineering expertise applied directly. Together, they were able to create unique system designs that satisfied both customers' critical telecommunications needs. Managing to "get closer to the customer" had been translated into two concrete successes.

New Structure to Support New Strategy

To make it easier for this customer-oriented service to work, the company's top management had created a new position, vice president of marketing and technology, thereby underscoring the emphasis on building closer connections between these two previously disparate functions. Within the new organization, McGruther was appointed director of a new unit comprised of forty engineers from the network planning department. This unit, Customer Network Design, had a crucial mandate: to provide technical telecommunications solutions for New York Telephone Company's top 200 customers.

The upstate successes had really pleased Bill McGruther and helped him to clarify the role he wanted his top engineers to play. But his engineers were uneasy about their new mission. In response to the idea of customer-focused projects, one engineer asserted, "Yes, we can do that on occasional projects, but that's no way to run an organization like this." Another confided, "I would like to try this approach, but I'd be surprised if the others buy into it." These people saw themselves as among the best telecommunications engineers in the world. Now they were being asked to play a marketing role. McGruther's challenge was to gear up his new customer network design group to operate in line with his vision, and he turned to the breakthrough strategy to do this.

McGruther created a project-focused organization. Twelve engineers were given the new title of "project manager." They would work on specific customer accounts and be responsible for revenue goals. This was a tremendous shift in role for the engineers. For the first time, success meant winning new business, not just designing a new communications network.

Bypassing all of the familiar and delaying preparation rituals that managers usually engage in at such turning points, McGruther selected a specific *result* as the goal to launch his group. It was not to train them in customer relations; it was not to do market research to discover the opportunities for the next five years; it was not to have seminars with other units in New York Telephone to define the role and mission of his group. The goal was: close ten sales contracts with the company's leading accounts, to generate $25 million in new revenue, on a scheduled basis, over the next six months.

The target prospects were drawn from an inventory of "requests for proposal" that, because of their unique requirements, had not been responded to earlier. Each of the twelve project managers was responsible for getting one new account (so that the overall goal would still be reached even if there were two misses) and for generating a particular amount of new revenue. The project managers were able to draw on a pool of technical people for support in developing proposals.

The project managers participated in a few work sessions in which they learned about the breakthrough strategy and developed step-by-step plans for such projects as the design of a local area network for Sears, an upgrade of Chemical Bank's ATM communications network, and an improvement to the functioning of the New York Lotto network. The project managers learned how to coordinate multifunctional teams from the sales, marketing, pricing, and legal departments. They also worked more closely with equipment vendors. Instead of accepting what vendors had to offer, they defined specific customer equipment requirements that had to be met.

This new strategy of bringing their technical expertise into close contact with the customer began to work almost at once. Within ten weeks, they had accomplished most of the overall goal (and they finished the rest well under deadline): ten wins and $25 million in new revenue. McGruther's group felt like winners. They became convinced that they could beat anyone in the marketplace, and they viewed the first ten projects as merely the beginning.

>> Simultaneous Strategy and Performance Improvements

Every company with ambitious, long-term strategic goals can find ways to translate them into successful, short-term action programs. Sometimes the strategies and action programs can be created simultaneously, as was done by Northern States Power.

In 1987, when Jim Howard took over as chief executive officer of Northern States Power in Minneapolis, he recognized that the electric power industry would be changing rapidly with the shift in the regulatory environment and the advent of new technology. He wanted to mobilize his management to agree on future directions and to get moving in those directions as quickly as possible. A strategic planning consultant had provided the company with a voluminous series of reports, containing as much as one would want to know about the industry. These thick reports did not, however, help the company crystallize its strategic directions.

Howard and his vice president for strategy, Bill Lynch, divided the top fifteen managers of the company into three teams. Each team was asked to identify (a) the major trends in the industry that they believed would most affect the future of the company; (b) the directions the company should establish to exploit opportunities ahead; and (c) the short-term strategic breakthrough projects that could produce some immediate benefits and get the company moving in the long-term direction.

At several half-day planning conferences, the three groups shared their conclusions and then consolidated their views. They reached consensus on the key trends that would affect Northern States Power, agreed on some of the major directions the company should move in, and also agreed on some immediate steps to take that would translate the long-term concepts into actions. A number of decisions that lay ahead would ultimately involve significant investment. But they were able to move at once on a new strategy for serving one of their largest customers, on an early retirement–cost reduction program, and on several other significant programs.

Howard accomplished all this in a few months. He and his team developed a vision of where they wanted to head, and they went ahead and acted on it. They agreed to hold periodic meetings to review progress and reassess their views of the industry and of their strategies.

Thus do successful short-term actions reflect strategic direction and contribute to ongoing strategic planning. Instead of being forced to make false choices between short-term and long-term issues, managers who learn to work on them simultaneously—as closely connected elements of competitive success—will be richly rewarded.

10

» *Management Development Through Management Achievement*

When a president realizes that the company's performance must improve but its managers don't seem to have the capacity to make it happen, what should he or she do? Wait and hope that eventually good managers will appear as others retire? Let a few of the poorest performers go and call the local headhunter? These strategies are very slow; while the faces may change, often the problems remain. It seems much more logical to try to increase the capability of the existing corps of managers. That was the challenge faced by Atlas Steels in the 1970s.

In Tracey, Quebec, Atlas had built one of the most sophisticated stainless steel mills in the world. Three years after it opened, however, the mill's actual output was very far from its projected output, and it was losing money.

Dozens of technological "fixes" were tried by the mill's own engineers and by a team of Japanese experts. It became clear that it was neither the mill's design nor its operating procedures that limited results, but how it was being run. Top management decided to shift tactics and to concentrate on strengthening its management team. They inaugurated a ten-week training program for twenty-five key middle managers, focusing on supervisory skills, union relations, and business economics—the last aimed mainly at helping mill managers and supervisors understand the importance of earning a return on the very large investment the company had made in the mill. Most senior managers share with Tracey's top management this great faith in the power of management education to produce improvement.

» *Leaps of Faith*

> Corporate Training has itself become big business. The American Society for Training and Development estimates companies are spending an astounding $30 billion a year on formal courses and training programs for workers. And that's only the tip of the iceberg. The institute figures it costs companies a further $180 billion annually for such unstructured training as supervision and learning on the job.
>
> —*Wall Street Journal*, August 5, 1986

What is it that inspires senior managers to invest so much in management education? First, there is the assumption that if managers are trained in a subject—say, better employee communications, or improved goal setting—they will go back and actually change how they communicate or set goals. The manager trained in "leadership" will lead differently. The manager trained in "problem-solving techniques" will apply the techniques to solve problems. This assumption is the first great leap of faith.

Top management, of course, is not interested in better goal setting or problem solving for their own sakes. They expect that improving these on-the-job behaviors will, in fact, lead directly to better bottom-line results. That is the second great leap of faith—the assumption that when managers do change their behavior as a result of their training, it will generate improvement in bottom-line results.

These two great leaps of faith often end with a thud. Despite the billions invested annually in management education, there is little empirical research that connects the huge investments with improved bottom-line results.

⟫ *Management Development: The Double Leap of Faith*

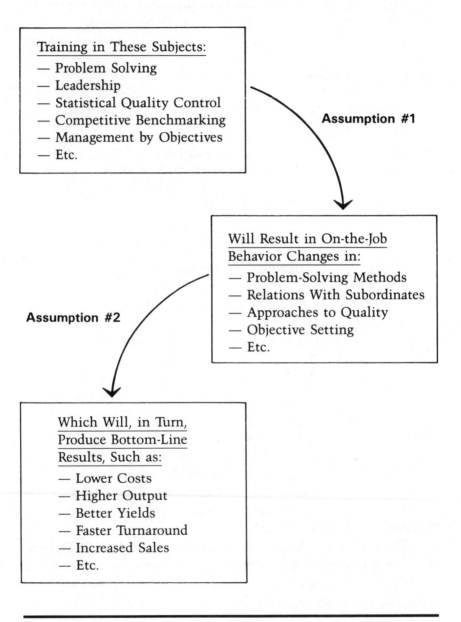

Training in These Subjects:
— Problem Solving
— Leadership
— Statistical Quality Control
— Competitive Benchmarking
— Management by Objectives
— Etc.

Assumption #1

Will Result in On-the-Job Behavior Changes in:
— Problem-Solving Methods
— Relations With Subordinates
— Approaches to Quality
— Objective Setting
— Etc.

Assumption #2

Which Will, in Turn, Produce Bottom-Line Results, Such as:
— Lower Costs
— Higher Output
— Better Yields
— Faster Turnaround
— Increased Sales
— Etc.

Thus, one company proudly asserts that it has trained thousands of supervisors and managers in a "seven-step problem-solving technique." No one can say to what extent the technique is being used, nor can they say how much better the results are where it is being used.

Atlas Steels' Tracy mill managers and supervisors were quite pleased by their development program. They felt the learnings were useful and relevant. They appreciated the recognition of their importance symbolized by the program. During the weeks following the course, however, the Tracy mill's steel output did not increase. Lifelong habits, anxiety-avoidance techniques, and traditional working methods, reinforced by the organization's cultural patterns, reasserted themselves when the managers went back to their jobs.

Exposing managers to typical management development programs is analogous to filling a stockroom with inventory. While managers are in training, they load up on a stock of insights, knowledge, and skills. It is expected that, thereafter, they will dip into that inventory and use it as needed. But as with materials in inventory, the full price is paid up front, and value is depleted as the stock sits around unused.

» *The Reinforcement of Reinforcement*

The wastefulness of this traditional store-it-up-now-and-use-it-later-maybe mode of training and development becomes obvious when managers contrast it with lessons they've taken in golf, tennis, or skiing. No one would sign up for a one-week classroom course in golf theory before being let out on the practice range to swing at a ball. No one would spend a week learning about the principles of skiing before making a turn on the hill. It is obvious that training in sports skills must be integrated with frequent application of techniques and the gradual internalization—or "grooving"—of new physical patterns.

Moreover, reinforcing success is critical to skill development. A golfer will try a new grip just so many times; if the ball keeps hooking, he'll go back to his old grip. Small, focused changes of technique are constantly tested and integrated into behavior patterns through successful experience. So logical for sports skills! And equally logical for managerial skills.

Greg Glashouser of Motorola's Training and Education Center named this practice-reinforcement approach, "just-in-time" training. Glashouser's term suggests that instead of loading managers with heavy infusions of information all at once, they are provided with increments, each aimed at facilitating some immediate progress on the job. Their training is put to use at once and reinforced by accomplishment, thus gradually, but permanently, affecting the manager's ongoing behavior patterns.

Because success is deliberately designed into the breakthrough project, it is an excellent vehicle for just-in-time management development. Managers are naturally reinforced in the use of the new approaches they've learned.

In the Crucible

No amount of training will change managerial patterns as much as they changed at Amstar's Chalmette refinery when teams set new output records. No training in goal setting, management by objectives, or "management of time" can have an impact comparable to the experience of the Calvert City managers when they increased the feed rates on their kilns by the "impossible" rate of 20 percent. The Atlas Steels mill managers learned a lot from their training sessions, but development of their capacity to move more stainless steel through the mill came only after their learning occurred on the job, in a series of results-oriented projects. They gradually increased the output of the mill and turned a loss into a profit.

When it comes to management training, it's time to put the horse before the cart. Instead of beginning with training and hoping that the trained managers will somehow produce improvement, consider the reverse, which is at the heart of the breakthrough strategy. The starting point is a demand from senior management, or an agreement on a critical result to be accomplished. Aim at that goal, and use training only to help the managers achieve it.

Let's see how this results-based management development works in practice.

›› *Just-in-Time Training at Morgan Guaranty Trust*

Bill Hayes, the administrative services department head, rose from his chair in the Morgan Guaranty Trust conference room at 40 Wall Street, walked forward, and turned to his audience. Before speaking, he scanned the forty-five faces in front of him, occasionally catching the eyes of a manager—one from Security, another from Systems, then one from the purchasing department, finally a nod to the manager of Restaurant Services. Many of them had spent their entire careers within their one function—mail service, micrographics, the print shop—becoming experienced and skilled in the technical details. The world of banking was changing rapidly in 1985, however, and Hayes needed aggressive, innovative managers to improve the uses of his $90 million budget and the performance of his 700 employees. He planned to "find" those new managers—through a development process—right in his own administrative services department. "Deregulation of the banking industry has meant tough, new competition," he began.

> Morgan has responded by decentralizing. Banking unit managers are now responsible for their own bottom-line performance. For the first time, Administrative Services is facing market pressures, like any other business. If we can't provide appropriate security services at an affordable price, if we can't get printing jobs done on time, our customers will look for those services outside the bank. And we'll be out of business. This means that we all need to ask some fundamental questions: What services should we be providing? Are there different ways to deliver those services? How can we be more effective?

Help in Responding to Demands

Hayes knew that the idea of doing this type of strategizing was radically new for many of the managers. "I don't expect all this to happen overnight," he assured his listeners.

> First, we'll work on some modest improvements in our current operations. When we have some success with that, we'll work on learning more about our customers and creating business plans.
>
> As you know, to get started, you will all attend a two-day workshop to begin our Performance Improvement Program. By the end of those two days, you will each have defined a measurable, short-term service improvement goal. I want to stress right now that the goals you select will be non-negotiable. You are responsible for making sure they are accomplished. The training you receive during the workshop will help you to structure a successful project.

Forty of Administrative Services' 700 employees were at the "officer" level and managed individual service sites—a restaurant, a mail department, a warehouse. Half of these forty officers participated in the first Performance Improvement Program (PIP) workshop in March 1985; the others soon followed.

The formal demand came from Bill Hayes in the form of a workshop preassignment.

MORGAN ADMINISTRATIVE SERVICES

» *Breakthrough Workshop Preassignment*

To: Participants in the Performance Improvement Workshop
From: William Hayes
Subject: Selecting Breakthrough Project Areas

Phase 1 of the Performance Improvement Program calls for each of you to design and carry out a modest breakthrough project to accomplish an important goal within 1–2 months. These projects are intended not only to achieve bottom-line results—but to serve as learning experiences in how to think more strategically and manage in more innovative ways.

Over the next few days, I would like each of you to select at least two potential improvement areas out of which you might be able to carve a breakthrough project.

(Continued)

Consider improvement areas that meet as many of these criteria as possible:

> Will involve improving relations with other Administrative Services functions and/or with other groups in the bank
> May involve potential applications of new technology to service delivery
> Will require you to delegate significant project responsibility to your staff
> Will require you to enlist cooperation and support of peers to accomplish important tasks

The workshop will be used to help you identify a specific, short-term breakthrough goal in one of these areas and to create the written project plans to accomplish this goal.

Please schedule a meeting with me to review the areas you have selected. Together we will choose one for planning and execution.

The purpose of a workshop such as this is to introduce the breakthrough strategy and launch the participants into action. Whenever it is essential to the achievement of the breakthrough goals, some just-in-time technical training can also be included. The workshop can be led by the sponsoring manager or by an internal facilitator familiar with the breakthrough concepts. The first workshops at Morgan Guaranty were led by an outside consultant.

Hidden Reserve and Zest

The managers were charged with getting better results without additional resources, so the workshop began with a discussion of the "hidden reserve." Everyone had personally experienced crises that mobilized high performance: the unannounced visit of an important banking official required that a banquet be put together in one-third the normal time; an "impossible" printing job was completed in time for Christmas vacation. Out of these experiences, the managers drew up a list of zest factors, which matched those mentioned so often by other groups.

Next, the managers focused the spotlight on their own hard-working business units, to identify areas of hidden reserve. Even managers who protest the loudest that they and their people are fully stretched have some awareness of the potentials. To bring this out, the administrative services managers filled out an opportunities questionnaire for their own groups.

》 *Opportunities*

Suppose in your organization that:

> 〉 All functions focused on the same few, compelling goals.
> 〉 Individuals began working much closer to their full potential.
> 〉 Redundant functions and people, unused reports, and other unnecessary work began to be phased out.
> 〉 Unproductive time spent in meetings, on the telephone, and in obtaining information was significantly reduced.
> 〉 People became more concerned about taking initiative and producing results, and less concerned about personal issues and politics.
> 〉 Different levels and different functions collaborated more effectively and quickly.
> 〉 More excitement, commitment, and enthusiasm was instilled in the work.

What kind of improvement might be achieved in output or results?

(A) Around 10 Percent ＿＿ (B) 10–30 Percent ＿＿
(C) 30–60 Percent ＿＿ (D) Over 60 Percent ＿＿

© Robert H. Schaffer & Associates 1986

When their responses—handed in anonymously—were tabulated on a flip chart, they were struck by what was revealed.

Opportunities for Improvement

Potential Improvement	Number of Managers Estimating This Potential in Their Own Unit
Around 10 Percent	2
10–30 Percent	7
30–60 Percent	4
Over 60 Percent	7

More than half the group saw 30 percent or greater improvement possibilities in their own units.

To see why all this potential remained bottled up, the group next looked at the institutionalized barriers to performance improvement and shared examples of how the barriers impeded progress in their own units.

These sessions established the basic premise of the breakthrough strategy: there is abundant hidden reserve in any group, and although the barriers keep it hidden, zest motivators liberate that reserve in crises. Instead of waiting for the next crisis or "impossible" deadline, the managers would now plan to engage the hidden reserve in an organized fashion to achieve the performance improvements that Bill Hayes had described as absolutely necessary.

Selecting and Refining Breakthrough Goals

Before the workshop, each of the managers, as directed in the preassignment, had selected one important performance improvement need. As a next step, each was to select and define a specific breakthrough goal. To illustrate how to do it, the group focused on the goal of Dorothy Jacobson, manager of the micrographics department. Her department transferred to microfilm information stored on computer tapes and then returned the much needed tapes to the various banking departments. She had a twenty-four-hour turnaround schedule that was often missed. Recently, the department had fallen as much as two weeks behind. Jacobson had come to the workshop with a general goal: improving the micrographics department's turnaround times.

With the breakthrough goal selection guidelines on the board—measurable, short-term, tough, yet achievable—people offered suggestions for what Jacobson's breakthrough goal might be. Some suggested "goals"—such as creating new microfilming procedures, training the staff, or improving coordination among the three shifts—that were steps toward a goal, but not goals themselves. Finally, with the help of the group, Jacobson decided on her breakthrough goal: to consistently achieve twenty-four-hour turnaround for work coming from one department, called "30 West Broadway," within five weeks.

With this one model goal defined, the participants broke into small groups and worked together to refine their own breakthrough goals and test them against the guidelines.

» *Sample Breakthrough Goals at Morgan Administrative Services*

> **Microfilm:** Eliminate backlog and achieve 24-hour turnaround of work from 30 West Broadway in 5 weeks.
> **Print Shop:** Improve turnaround time of printing jobs 20 percent in 8 weeks.
> **Food Services:** Food portions to meet standards 90 percent of the time in 6 weeks—with focus on high-cost items.
> **Security:** Implement "block watch" program in 30 Broad Street in 4 weeks, and reduce incidents by 80 percent within 12 weeks.
> **Mail:** Develop controls and procedures for registered mail in 8 weeks—to increase security and service.
> **Library:** Verify usefulness of 100 periodicals in 6 weeks, and cancel subscriptions if unused.
> **Purchasing:** Reduce time needed to provide purchase analysis from 12 person-days to 8 person-days in 8 weeks.

Practice in Making a Demand

Every manager in the room was going to have to ask his or her people to make a major step-up in performance. It was inevitable they would have to deal with some resistance and some anxiety, both in their people and in themselves. As the final activity of the day, therefore, the managers practiced how to convey their expectations and how to deal with the reactions.

Dorothy Jacobson participated in one "role-play"—testing how she would inform her assistant, John Pallidino, what her expectations of him would be in achieving the twenty-four-hour turnaround. Jacobson's partner in the role-play came up with all the responses that Pallidino might make: "We're already working very hard." "I can't see how we can do it and keep up with all the other work we have." "We'll never make it without more maintenance support for our equipment." Dorothy's uneasiness was obvious—she was reluctant to put too much pressure on her people—but she hung in during the role-play and kept pressing her demand.

Great oaks from little acorns grow. Developing the capacity of managers like Dorothy Jacobson to ask for more and to get it is the acorn of widespread performance improvement in organizations.

Project Assignments and the Written Work Plan

The second day of the workshop began with work on project assignments, the written document that conveys the expectations for the breakthrough project. "Writing a project assignment forces you to clearly define—in one or two pages—exactly what you want accomplished," began the consultant working with the group. "If several people—or functions—are involved in the project, the written assignment ensures that they will all be be working toward the same goal."

The managers then worked on developing the actual project assignments they would use to launch their projects. As part of that exercise, they had to identify clearly who the key players were to be and the role of each one. Then they had to decide how they would work with these people and what decisionmaking and review meetings would be required. Even managers whose projects at first seemed to involve just a few people found that careful clarifying of their plans smoked out many issues that required resolution.

In Dorothy Jacobson's case, three shift supervisors would each have a role to play in developing ideas and in working with their people. Jacobson also thought she would have to involve people from the target department, 30 West Broadway, and possibly the messengers who transported the computer tapes and the people who provided computer maintenance. As she considered the various groups and individuals who would be involved, a more detailed picture of her project began to take shape.

Creating the written project work plan was the next step in the workshop. The managers drafted their plans and then reviewed their drafts with each other, according to the guidelines outlined in Chapter 6. To test their work plans, they asked each other questions like these.

❯❯ *Testing Your Work Plan*

1. Does it contain all of the basic plan ingredients—accountabilities, steps, start and end dates, measure of progress?
2. Does it include steps to gain the commitment of people who must contribute to, or can affect, its success?
3. Does it identify the areas of greatest challenge or concern? Have ways to deal with these challenges been thoroughly explored?
4. Does the project seem to be loaded for success on the basis of this plan? Are there any alternative strategies that might increase the chances of success?
5. Are there people with whom the plan should be reviewed or discussed, even though they are not directly involved in the work? Have steps for doing so been included?

Finding Time to Manage Improvement:
The Presidential Assignment

These Morgan managers had asserted—as so many do—that day-to-day pressures were so great, they would be hard-pressed to find time to work on their projects. This was the final subject of the workshop, using what I call the "presidential assignment." They were each asked to consider this question: "What would you do if the president of the bank personally invited you, on a voluntary basis only, to work on a special project with him? It would take about a day a week, and he tells you to accept only if you feel you can keep your regular job going during the three or four months of the project."

When the workshop leader asked who would accept the assignment, every hand went up. After complaining that they could barely find time to come to the workshop, they were all saying they could take a day out of every week and still get their jobs done. That provoked a good laugh in the group.

"If I *had* to do it, I'd find a way," explained one person. "I couldn't pass up an opportunity for that kind of development and exposure. I'd delegate my less critical work," said another. "I'd train my people to take over some tasks, and find shortcuts for others," said a third.

"Your comments illustrate the point of this exercise perfectly," said the workshop leader. "Just as in a crisis or emergency, *having to do it* provides the energizing force to make things happen in ways we don't think about ordinarily."

He then asked the group to choose three specific tasks they could gain some time on, starting the next day—one from each of these categories:

1. One task you always do that you can eliminate
2. One task that you can do in half the time
3. One task you always do that you can delegate to someone else

Nobody had trouble identifying one of each, and they shared their ideas:

"I always read all my mail every day. I could ask my secretary to sort out what I don't need to see."

"I always look over all reports that go to other departments. I could tell people to send me only the reports they feel I should read."

And dozens of more ideas came out of the woodwork.

Everyone agreed that the workshop had done much to prepare them to take on their projects. But at the dinner that night for the workshop "graduates," Dorothy Jacobson reflected a concern she shared with most of her colleagues. She confided that she was worried about reaching her "non-negotiable" goal. "This is just one more demand on top of everything else," she said, "and my people are already working so hard. I don't even want to think about what I'll be facing tomorrow morning, after two days away from the department."

Back to the "Real" World

The scene that greeted Dorothy Jacobson as she walked through the door of the micrographics department the next morning was just what she had predicted. "How's it going?" she asked the night shift supervisor. "Bad," he responded. "We had a couple of systems down last night. And some tapes arrived late, so we never got to them."

Even before removing her coat, Jacobson was involved in reprioritizing the day's work. That was followed by an emergency having to do with some badly scratched microfilm. Next came phone calls from other departments asking about their missing computer tapes. The two-day work session already seemed far in the past. It had taken her no time at all to become overwhelmed by the "busyness" of her job.

Sitting at her desk with a cup of coffee in hand, three hours after her arrival at Micrographics, Jacobson began to reach for the mail and phone messages that had piled up during her absence—and suddenly stopped. Instead, she reached into her briefcase and took out her breakthrough project work plan. She slowly read the goal written across the top: "Twenty-four-hour turnaround for 30 West Broadway in five weeks." It struck her how easily she had fallen back into fire fighting after two days of thoughtful planning. Remembering that she was committed to produce the results, she reread the goal and work plan and said to herself, "I'd better get started."

Management Development Means Making It Happen

Jacobson met her assistant, John Pallidino, in the Micrographics conference room. The moment had come when she would test what she had learned about making a demand and sticking to it. She had sent Pallidino the project assignment memo the previous afternoon, explaining the 30 West Broadway project and describing his responsibilities. "Because 30 West Broadway has been such a thorn in our side," Jacobson began, "I have decided that getting it under control will be the first step in achieving twenty-four-hour turnaround for all our work."

"This project," questioned Pallidino, "is to be done only with the people I already have?"

"There will be no staff increases," Jacobson firmly responded. "I need a draft action plan tomorrow, in written form. I need the steps you intend to take, assignment of responsibilities, and time frames for completion."

They called in Josie Sicignano, the first shift supervisor, and continued discussing what they needed to accomplish during the next five weeks. Once again, Jacobson's resolve was challenged. "There's no way we can do this," said Sicignano, "not without some additional people. We just don't have enough help. There will be an explosion when we tell people about this."

Jacobson had always been concerned about putting too much pressure on her people, and she felt herself wanting to give way, to ease off a bit on the demand. But the workshop practice paid off. "I understand that this seems difficult," she told Sicignano, "but we're going to take it one step at a time and work together. Expectations have been raised. We're not working at the same level anymore."

Training Proceeds With the Project

As her project proceeded, Jacobson continued to receive training and guidance from the consultant and support from her fellow workshop participants. Each week, groups of managers met to discuss their progress and share their ideas—ideas that were put to use to keep the projects moving ahead.

Jacobson met regularly with her assistants. She defined a new role for one person; as "work flow coordinator," that person tracked the flow of each job throughout the three shift operations. She created a temporary structure, the "supervisor action committee," which met to resolve conflicts between the shifts. She designed a wall chart to track the results of all work coming from 30 West Broadway.

After just several weeks, the atmosphere in Micrographics had already begun to change. Josie Sicignano, so skeptical at first, summed up how she felt. "There's not as much tension on all of us. When I arrive in the morning, the shelves aren't so packed full. So we can work at a normal speed, instead of running around like crazy people." Pushing through to the first success was increasing confidence. Jacobson and her supervisors were becoming managers instead of fire fighters.

The Developmental Rewards of Victory

On her project due date, Dorothy Jacobson walked into her manager's office and presented the results: 30 West Broadway was being turned around on a twenty-four-hour basis every day—they had accomplished the goal. She felt a lot of pride in the way her people had responded, and also in how she had developed as a manager. Before she had been overwhelmed by the "busyness" of her job; now she could confidently look forward to the step-by-step achievement of her long-range goal: twenty-four-hour turnaround for *all* Micrographics work.

And so a few days later, it was back to the Micrographics conference room for Jacobson, Pallidino, and Sicignano. They were there to launch the next phase of the improvement effort: twenty-four-hour turnaround for work from the custody department.

Development Continues in Administrative Services

Dorothy Jacobson's first projects in Micrographics were just one example of the many successful projects carried out in Administrative Services by the original forty managers. Over the months, as their operations became better controlled, they moved to a next step in their development as managers: creating business plans. First, they interviewed their internal "customers" and identified the most important improvements they needed to make in their services. Then, using this information and a few just-in-time training sessions on developing business plans, they identified specific goals for the improvement of their services over the coming year. Each goal in their plans was tied to specific breakthrough projects that their people would carry out.

During the next several years, over 125 managers and supervisors participated in the results-oriented workshop process and took the lead in their own improvement projects. Dorothy Jacobson and some of the other "veterans" served as resources for less experienced people who were launching their first breakthrough projects. As services were improved and expanded, the department reduced staff by eighty-five people (who were shifted to other positions in the bank) and saved millions of dollars in operating expenses.

Because Bill Hayes had chosen to connect management development directly with business improvement, each new project strengthened the managerial ranks of his department. His people all understand that constant improvement is the way of life at Morgan Administrative Services. Management *development* and management *achievement* are continuously linked together in a *never-ending* process.

11
>> *Quality Improvement by Improving Quality*

It is no great revelation to say that high quality requires the right technology and design support; concern and interest on the part of employees; alertness by purchasing professionals; skill and sophistication by quality professionals; and the right work methods, tools, measurements, and processes. Often overlooked in the welter of details, however, is the fact that good quality requires consummate management skill in blending these ingredients into a desired result.

>> The Hidden Factory

AES Data Company's managers developed a keen appreciation for this. In 1985, this Montreal-based manufacturer of word processors faced an increasingly competitive marketplace in which even companies with well-established product lines could survive only by reducing costs and delivering products of the highest quality. AES had recently carried out a major reorganization to reduce costs, consolidating plants and reducing staff. It was much less clear, however, how it was going to get control over its quality problems. The inspection, rework, and scrap costs required in order to ship perfect machines to the customer were excessive.

The director of quality control, Armand Dufresne, described the procedures to correct defects:

> When we identify a faulty component, we bring it to the attention of Engineering. They take it from there and, after doing an analysis, write a report. Then they pass the report on to Purchasing or Manufacturing, where the problem is supposed to be resolved. But if Manufacturing doesn't know how to respond to the report, they might set it aside or undertake their own study. Or, if they disagree, they might send it back to Engineering with a memo. Often the different functions do not work closely with each other, and follow-up is not coordinated.

As Dufresne talked, it became evident that accountability both for quality assurance and quality improvement was dispersed widely. There was no single person in any of the operations departments whose job it was to make sure that a defect was corrected, and that it would not happen again.

Thus, while most of the managers in AES were people of good will who really wanted their company to succeed, the money being spent on quality was not producing the needed results. AES shared this frustration with many other American companies. In his book, *Total Quality Control*, Armand Feigenbaum sums up the toll exacted by shortcomings in quality:

> Even in many highly organized factories, there now exists what might be called a "hidden plant"—amounting to 15 percent to as much as 40 percent of productive capacity.... This is the proportion of plant capacity that exists to rework unsatisfactory parts, to replace products recalled from the field, or to retest and reinspect rejected units.[1]

Feigenbaum's 15 to 40 percent is just another ingredient in the hidden reserve—paid for but squandered.

---

1. Armand V. Feigenbaum. *Total Quality Control*, 3rd edition (New York: McGraw-Hill, 1983), pp. 46–47.

Good Programs Alone Are Not Sufficient

After too many years of insufficient attention to quality American management began to "get religion" in the 1970s and 1980s. Using Japanese companies and the experts associated with Japan's success as models, American companies have tried to make the great leap to improved quality. Most of the investment has gone into four distinct areas:

1. *Technology:* Introducing statistical quality control, better measurements, testing, inspection, and analytical techniques
2. *Training and Education:* Teaching managers, supervisors, and employees more about quality improvement methods and procedures
3. *Employee Involvement Techniques:* Tapping into the contributions that employees might make to quality improvement
4. *Awareness and Communications:* Sharpening people's understanding of the importance of quality with awareness sessions, speeches, inspirational messages, banners and posters—and including quality goals in annual goals assessments

While these ingredients are essential to successfully improving quality, too often managers assume that they are sufficient; that if the right dosage of these ingredients is administered to the patient, high quality will result. It won't. Quality is too vulnerable to all the invisible barriers. These remarks will sound familiar:

"The parts we get from the vendors often don't fit."

"If the guys in Development Engineering spent any time out here in the shop, they would never come up with these weird designs."

"My boss talks quality—until we're late with a delivery."

When all their quality programs fail to achieve sufficient results, as they often do, managers may conclude that they haven't been investing enough. So they redouble their efforts, invest more money, and install more programs, hoping that somehow, in some way, superior quality will emerge—like the lost city of Atlantis—out of the mist. What they need to understand is that quality programs may support the management initiatives that are needed to improve quality, but they cannot substitute for those initiatives.

» *Shifting Focus from Quality Programs to Quality Results*

What people need to learn is that quality, however defined and measured, is a performance issue. As such, accountable managers must be assigned to produce quality results. Armand Dufresne came to appreciate the power of this results-first concept. Disappointing results had convinced him that new quality systems and procedures alone would not produce the necessary improvement. There needed to be an accountability for improving quality results that cut across all functions.

Dufresne and the AES operations vice president, Don Nichols, considered their options for establishing that accountability: A restructuring of the quality function? A quality "mission statement" signed off on by each function? Workshops to enhance communications? They finally agreed to initiate a quality step, but with a new twist: Armand Dufresne himself would take personal responsibility for making an immediate improvement in quality results. And it didn't take much discussion to agree on where to begin.

Both Dufresne and Nichols were troubled by a glaring symbol in their plant of the quality problem—the so-called "bad parts quarantine" area. This corner of the production floor had been fenced in as a temporary holding area for rejected parts, to keep them out of the production area. It was costly enough to find bad parts on inspection, but they wanted to be absolutely certain that no bad part would ever be built into the product. By that time, quarantined parts had overflowed the fenced-in area. Improving this highly visible situation could establish the momentum required for larger changes.

Sharpening the Goal

Dufresne met with the top managers of Production, Design Engineering, Purchasing, Manufacturing, and Incoming Inspection, to select a first goal. Each functional manager presented his own views on why the number of parts in quarantine was so high. Incoming inspection was too strict. Vendors weren't able to meet the company's high quality standards. There were no clear guidelines for the disposition of rejected materials, and so they sat in quarantine. Eventually, Dufresne suggested a shift: "Instead of analyzing all the causes and trying to find who is responsible for them," he said, "let's define a specific goal we can work towards." This was a new concept.

Dufresne suggested how the task force might select its goal:

> The most useful step we can take is to recycle the good, reparable parts sitting out there in quarantine costing us money. We need to identify and repair these parts. Then we need to get rid of the rest and make sure that the number of quarantined materials begins shrinking. Let's start by concentrating on a few parts and getting them out of quarantine."

They analyzed the contents of the quarantine area and generated a list of "hot items." Hot items were parts that (1) were rejected on a recurring basis, (2) were essential to production, and (3) carried a high dollar value. The team discovered that the top eight hot items alone had a value of $630,000, about half of the total $1.2 million of quarantined material. That led to their selection of a first-step goal: reduce the value of quarantined parts by $600,000 within two months, and do it in ways that would stick. The words "quality improvement" now had a very specific, results-focused meaning to the task force members.

The task force took one of the eight parts at a time and made an analysis of all its reported defects. For instance, drive motors were being rejected because they were "too noisy." Team members went to the engineering department and listened to a number of rejected motors. There didn't seem to be any clear definition of "noisy"; apparently, the "standard" was at the discretion of each inspector. In response, the team issued assignments for subprojects to managers in the various functions. Engineering was to define clearly the quality requirements for drive motors by a certain date. Purchasing was assigned to make sure that the vendor understood the requirements. Quality Control was asked to work with each vendor's quality control department to standardize testing procedures. At each task force meeting, progress toward reducing the number of rejected drive motors to zero was reviewed. Work plans were updated. The process was repeated for each of the eight hot items.

Get It Down and Keep It Down

While working to improve the results on the eight hot items, the task force also streamlined basic procedures for processing quarantined materials. They agreed on steps for removing rejected parts from quarantine and from the plant. They expedited the processing of quality reports, revised standards for incoming parts, and communicated those standards to suppliers. They clarified responsibilities for dealing with vendors. But no matter how good any procedural change sounded, before agreeing to it they would ask: Will doing this make a contribution toward immediate improvements in performance? Will it prevent future quality problems from occurring?

Within two months, the focused efforts had paid off. People could see that all rejected parts now fit within the quarantine fences. The value of rejected stock sitting idle had been reduced by more than the $600,000 goal.

The enthusiasm and confidence generated by this initial success encouraged the team to select a second breakthrough project, this one to be focused on rejects originating in the manufacturing process. The goal was to reduce the reject rate of printed circuit boards from 21 percent to 10 percent within six weeks. A new quality improvement action team initiated a series of projects, which met the goal in the allocated time.

As these initial successes produced increasing quality and cost improvement, Armand Dufresne took steps to institutionalize the breakthrough approach to quality. In work sessions with his people, specific and measurable quality goals to be achieved during the following quarter were defined. Progress on the plans was then reviewed on a quarterly basis, and the next quarter's goals were selected.

Starting from one project that improved quality results, Dufresne had evolved an ongoing, results-oriented quality process based on close collaboration among functions. And all of this occurred in a span of time that would hardly have been long enough for the more customary approaches to have designed all the training programs and to have processed all the people through them.

The AES case shows that step-by-step, measurable improvements of quality point the way to the larger strategic and procedural changes that need to be made in the management of quality. Thus, in addition to immediate paybacks, the more fundamental changes needed to sustain AES as a high-quality, low-cost producer were discovered and institutionalized.

Trapped by Old Assumptions

Despite all the evidence that quality results can be achieved quickly—not as a band-aid, but as a solid step toward continuing improvement— the "invest in programs today and results will come tomorrow" mentality dominates the quality field. It is encouraged by quality consultants, by academic writers, and by the popular business media. For example, in the June 8, 1987 special issue of *Business Week* devoted to quality, an editorial writer asserts:

> Truly improving quality ... frequently carries a steep
> up-front cost. Unwilling to spend money to save money,
> some executives are resisting quality-enhancing measures.
> But the initial investment in equipment and training is
> well worth making. *Eventually*, the savings ... far exceed
> the costs of a quality program. (Emphasis added)

The idea that big, up-front investments are necessary to improve quality reinforces all the wrong ideas. It implies that people are already "doing the best they can," given their current resources. This attitude encourages them to not take responsibility for improving quality—because the big quality programs will be coming along to solve the problem.

It is time to reverse the order, to escape from the "begin with programs" mentality. Start getting some quality improvements and savings right away. Then, as at AES Data Company, management will become increasingly certain, after they have had some tangible success, about what technological or educational investments are needed for further progress. Moreover, the savings from earlier phases can be used to fund the later capital-intensive phases.

» *Selecting Quality Breakthrough Goals: Back to Basics*

The effort to achieve high quality—not only in products but in every aspect of performance—is a microcosm of what's needed to become competitive. Time and again, I've seen companies use the disciplined, results-first framework of the breakthrough strategy to successfully meet this challenge.

In deciding where to start, keep in mind the guidelines for selecting a breakthrough project:

1. *Begin with an urgent and compelling goal.* Company-wide efforts to train people and get everybody "quality-conscious" almost guarantee that people will not be working on urgent and compelling goals. The "urgent and compelling" motivation will work only if the people who are being asked to improve quality can recognize the urgency.
2. *Set a first-step subgoal.* All too often, quality is worked on as a long-term, never-ending activity. The short-term subgoal makes it possible for people to have a clear endpoint in sight and to enjoy the reinforcement of quick success.
3. *The subgoal should be discrete and measurable,* focused on a real bottom-line result. The more ambitious the company's quality improvement program, the more this guideline is usually violated.
4. *The project must be based on existing readiness.* Massive quality improvement efforts rarely consider the different levels of interest, concern, ability, and response capacity within a company. Only by making sure that each group selects the steps that people are ready and willing to undertake can one begin to expect real improvements.
5. *The goal should be achievable with available resources and authority.* Accepting and acting on the idea that quality can be improved with what is already in place may be the single most difficult shift of thinking for managers to make. Yet it is essential; they have to be liberated from the view

that extensive training, new systems, better tools and measurements, and employee involvement programs must all precede real quality improvement.

Consider the quality improvement efforts in your company, and see how overlooking even one of these "select for success" criteria can sabotage the accomplishment of measurable results. AES at first did not have specific goals—beyond making sure their products were perfect. The change came only when they launched a results-first attack. Starting with the urgent need to reduce quarantined bad parts, they set the first-step subgoal: reduce quarantined scrap by half. That was certainly a discrete and measurable goal. The people who had to make it happen designed the remedial steps, so every action plan was based on what they themselves were ready to do. As to available resources and authority, since each of the groups involved knew that it would have to accomplish its assigned results, each group defined steps it knew it could take.

The Moncks Corner plant of Uniroyal had the challenging task of producing precision-machined rubber timing belts for the automobile industry. As described in Chapter 3, when other efforts had failed to solve a quality problem, plant management seized on a "quality circles" approach. Considerable investment was made in training and in conducting weekly employee meetings. These get-togethers allowed employees and supervisors to share perspectives on plant operations and on quality problems. They did not, however, improve quality.

Eventually, they switched to a results-first focus. Their most serious quality problems were occurring on Line 7. In June, one type of problem alone, "full slab cure defects," caused over forty serious defects a week. One week there were over sixty-six defects. Vital shipments needed in automobile assembly were being delayed—a sacrilege in automobile manufacture.

The production manager and the shift supervisors on Line 7, working with groups of employees, set a breakthrough goal of thirty defects per week, maximum. Together, they worked out specific steps they could take that would help them reach that goal—checking temperatures more regularly, for example. By the end of July, they not only reached the goal but bettered it. With newfound confidence, they then boldly cut the goal in half: to fifteen defects per week, maximum. And they began achieving that goal, too.

The handful of supervisors and employees involved in the first Moncks Corner project made use of almost all of the breakthrough strategy work practices in ways that taught new skills and management techniques. As they succeeded in their first subgoal—reducing full slab cure defects—the supervisors on Line 7 began to use the same technique on other defects, and overall quality on Line 7 began to improve. Meanwhile, the plant's production manager encouraged supervisors on other lines to use the methodology, and overall plant quality gradually improved. The initial focus on one breakthrough goal was not made at the expense of all the other goals, but was made, rather, to their benefit.

If, within the framework of an overall corporate quality goal, managers begin to identify and carry out a series of breakthrough projects in their own areas, quality improvement can become a results-focused activity at the center of a corporatewide improvement effort. The work disciplines of the breakthrough strategy create the basis for constantly expanding improvements. Let's see how one Allied-Signal Corporation plant used a first project as a springboard to plantwide progress.

» *New Quality Tool for Allied-Signal: Two School Buses*

"The first thing we're going to do is hire two school buses," said Bill Mathias, plant manager of the Allied-Signal Corporation's home furnishings fiber mill in Columbia, South Carolina. His production and quality control managers responded with puzzled looks. They had come to his office to discuss quality improvement. The Columbia mill, which produced nylon fibers used by manufacturers of carpets, had been receiving numerous customer complaints.

For several years in the early 1980s, despite many quality improvement efforts—training programs, extensive laboratory testing, and the formation of a quality control department— they continued to be plagued by defects that caused production problems in their customers' carpet mills. Quality awareness, quality knowledge, and quality activity weren't being translated into quality results. This was severely hampering the Columbia mill in its battle for market share with its two sophisticated competitors, DuPont and Monsanto.

A Lesson in Quality

"We'll hire two school buses," Mathias said again, " and go to visit a customer. Our people need to see firsthand the effects of poor quality." A few days later, forty supervisors and hourly workers traveled to a customer's mill for some real-life quality training. The customer's mill manager took the group around and showed them the consequences of defects in the fibers: machines down and bins full of material to be reworked. "Know what happened to that machine?" a foreman asked. "Drips of nylon on the fibers fouled up the needles."

The visitors asked which problems were most common and which were the most costly. The mill manager contrasted Allied-Signal's product with that of a competing supplier. This direct evidence of their own manufacturing shortcomings was having a powerful effect on the group. It was obvious from the animated discussions that began at the customer's mill and continued during the bus ride home that a new sense of urgency for quality improvement was developing.

An Immediate First Step

After the tour, Bill Mathias discussed his options for a quality improvement project with a consultant who was assisting in launching the quality effort. "Now that my people are ready to go, where do we begin?" The consultant described how a breakthrough project could be a model for improving quality one step at a time. He suggested that Mathias give a clear assignment to the quality control manager to work with the operating people in getting some projects launched that would actually make some measurable improvements in quality. One defect in particular, "drips,"—coagulations of nylon on the fibers,— had been the subject of many complaints during the mill visit. "If you have any way to measure progress on that defect," the consultant commented, "it would be a natural starting point."

Later that day, Mathias met once again with his production and quality control managers. "Do we have any good way of measuring how we're doing with drips?" he asked.

"We've got one spinning machine—No. 806—where we recently started keeping some statistics," the production manager told him. "We installed a 'drip counter,' a little mechanical device that touches the stream of fiber coming out of the spinerette. A mechanical arm flips every time a drip hits it. It's not fancy, but it gives a good count."

"That's where we start then," said Mathias, turning to the quality control manager. "On No. 806." Not with a massive drip-avoidance training program. Not by replacing the crude drip counter with a more sophisticated instrument. Not by installing measuring devices on the other machines. "Meet with the foreman for that machine," he directed, "and see what kind of goal we can set for reduction of drips. When we get some results there, we can move on to the other machines."

The quality control manager and the foreman for No. 806 set the ambitious goal of completely eliminating drips within two months. The consultant provided the framework for managing the project and for involving those people with contributions to make. Quality engineers were assigned to provide technical assistance. Over the weeks, they began to test a variety of actions, no one of which was all that novel.

First, they worked more systematically on cleaning the spinerettes through which the fiber flowed. Operators charted drip counter measurements regularly; if the frequency of drips increased, the machine was stopped and cleaned. They found, and eliminated, contaminents in the incoming polymer material. They discovered surprisingly wide variations in temperature, which changed the fiber viscosity, and they developed some techniques to control these fluctuations. They were encouraged when they saw the drip count decreasing toward the goal, slowly but consistently.

Two months later—at the project completion deadline—the quality control manager presented his report at a plant management meeting. "The fiber coming out of No. 806 is as pure as the driven snow," he said. "It's the best fiber anyone has ever produced." Then he smiled, listening to the first round of applause he had ever received for his work.

Two Customers—Two Defects

Bill Mathias then asked the quality control manager to take the process one step further—to reduce other defects by working directly with additional customers. Mathias identified two key customers and asked the quality control manager to choose two defects causing trouble for those customers. "We'll call it the 2-by-2 Project," he said. "Two defects and two customers." His idea was to use the project not only to improve quality within the Columbia mill, but also to strengthen customer relationships by demonstrating the company's real commitment to reducing customer operating costs. During this phase, they extended their work on drips to other machines while also focusing on a second defect called "fusion."

The two customers were informed of this special effort, and when they agreed to participate, Mathias sent several engineers to their mills to determine how the fiber could be made to run better. At the outset of this effort, they discovered a new barrier. The mill and its customer didn't have a common language for discussing quality improvement problems. "This last shipment had a bad burr problem," explained a supervisor in the customer mill. "Burrs? What's a burr?" asked the Allied engineer.

It turned out to be the customer's word for "drips." The 2-by-2 team and the quality laboratory manager built a "sample board"— a rogue's gallery of the different kinds of defects, with the agreed-upon name under each. This provided a common set of terms. Each small step, such as the sample board, made it easier to track quality results and to strengthen the customer-supplier relationship. Over the course of several months, fibers made in the Columbia mill with either a drip or fusion defect dropped from about 10 percent of the mill's output to virtually zero.

Persistent Quality Improvement

Once the mill management and work force saw what they could accomplish with a step-by-step process for quality improvement, they stopped waiting for the big quality fix from on high and changed their whole approach. They began to see opportunities in every operation and enjoyed the challenge of each new project. Since that first breakthrough project, they have attacked each stage in the production process with a continuing series of incremental quality goals. New measurements have been developed. Production supervisors have been trained to work with their people on both quality and productivity goals. The cumulative impact of these steps and the persistent pursuit of higher quality targets has lifted performance.

Today, the percentage of output rated as "first quality"— which Allied-Signal's Columbia mill can sell at a premium price—exceeds 96 percent. The largest increment achieved in one year alone, from 92 percent to 96 percent, was worth over $4 million to the mill that year. The cost of all this progress? Some very hard work and—oh, yes— the cost of chartering two school buses to go 120 miles.

Earlier in this chapter, we listed some of the popular programs and technologies that are now being employed to advance quality. But the attempt to improve quality by pumping in these programs, in the absence of demands, accountability, incremental goals, detailed work plans, measurements, and the other key management practices, can often be futile. On the other hand, as managers achieve a succession of quality improvements, they become much clearer about where and how their efforts should be directed. Moreover, they become more confident in their ability to manage the experts who are providing the quality improvement technology.

A far-reaching corporate effort in quality can indeed be generated— with every aspect of that effort marked by the identification of specific short-term goals, which can then be enhanced by the introduction of quality technologies and systems to support results achievement. As managers learn to accomplish these goals, and as increasingly sophisticated technology to support the process is introduced, each function can select the breakthrough goals that are most relevant to doing a better job—goals measured not by the unit's internal criteria, but by what customers in other functions and in the outside world desire.

PART IV

The High-Performance, Change-Oriented Organization

12
>> Putting It All Together

After twenty-five-plus years of consulting—working with almost every kind of industry in North America, at every level and with every function—there is no doubt in my mind that the basic motivation to do a far superior job is out there. In companies, government, social agencies, hospitals, and schools, the overwhelming majority of people have a basic desire to be part of a winning team and to enjoy the pride of accomplishment.

They not only have the desire, they have the capacity. When given the opportunity—whether through organized effort or through an unexpected crisis—they prove time and time again that they are capable of rising to meet great challenges. Unfortunately, a combination of historical, cultural, and psychological barriers, defective work patterns and procedures, and only the dimmest vision on the part of senior managers of what might be possible, have kept organizations from capitalizing on all this latent capacity.

Instead, somewhat frustrated by the comparative success of other companies and other countries, managers have poured into their organizations tremendous investments in new capital equipment, facilities, and computer hardware and software. They have reorganized. They have trained managers. They've tried to get employees involved. They've read dozens of books and articles and attended seminars, trying to draw lessons from what the most successful companies are doing.

In this book, I have highlighted one critical dimension of the effort that they have overlooked: developing the basic capacity of their organizations at every level to get work done and to get it done well. And I have suggested how to begin to come to grips with that weakness in fundamental performance capability—through short-term achievement. We've seen how initial breakthrough projects can facilitate development of the management skills and working methods needed for constant improvement, how they free managers to experiment with new strategic directions, and how they can become the vehicles by which the organization absorbs and exploits new systems, new methods, and new technologies.

The breakthrough strategy sets in motion a step-by-step learning process that ripples through every part of an organization and can even involve customers and suppliers. Long-range goals, though kept in view, are temporarily put aside while people work on what they are ready and able to do immediately. With each new project, managers increase their respect for the power of the basic management disciplines and expand their ability to use staff experts and technological innovations to support progress.

As Fast as You Want to Go

Yes, but there is so much to accomplish! The world is changing rapidly, and every day seems to bring new crises for any organization that's not keeping pace. Some managers have challenged the concept of the breakthrough strategy: "We don't have time for step-by-step changes around here. We need to make things happen fast."

The implication that step-by-step, deliberate, managed change is necessarily slow is not correct. It's hard work. It's frequently stressful. It's demanding, both mentally and physically. But slow? Not necessarily. It can be as fast as you want to make it.

The story in Chapter 1 of the turnaround at Bell Canada illustrates the point. A major conference of eighty senior managers launched the effort. Performance improvement projects were then organized in all six of the company's operating areas. Substantial savings were realized within months of the start-up. Success in one department opened the way for similar performance improvements in other functions. The process spread quickly to the entire operations force of 40,000 people.

During the few years just before the process was initiated, Bell Canada's work force had been increasing at a rate parallel to its increases in work load. During the next two years, however, while the work load continued to increase at approximately 15 percent a year, the size of the work force actually declined. This represented an improvement in overall productivity of well over 30 percent in about two years. During this period, the Montreal area of Bell Canada, for example, went from being one of the lowest rated areas in North America to being one of the best. Slow? It is rare for companies of this size to achieve such results in two years.

≫ The Transformation of PPG Industries' Fiber Glass Products

In earlier chapters, I've concentrated on the individual elements of improvement—achieving a first breakthrough, mulitiplying the projects, piloting new strategic directions, providing technical support, developing managers—to highlight the unique requirements of each task.

As top management orchestrates all the elements of the strategy, however, it can bring them together into an overall process that can fundamentally change the way work gets done throughout the organization. That is just what Frank Green, vice president of PPG Industries, Fiber Glass Products, had to do.

In 1984 he became deeply concerned about his Reinforced Plastics Group. His business was like many others that had been successful for years in one set of market conditions, but suddenly found themselves confronting a very different set of conditions.

He realized that continuing to operate in the mode that had made his business so successful in the past could cause it to fail in the future. He needed to find ways to change directions radically and quickly. Having grown and prospered in a steadily expanding industry, however, the organization had very little experience in formulating major strategic shifts or in carrying them out. That was his dilemma.

Twenty-Five Years of Success

When it was founded in 1952, PPG Fiber Glass was at the forefront of a technological revolution. Its Reinforced Plastics Group produced fiberglass that, when mixed with plastic, formed a material whose high strength, light weight, and resistance to corrosion made it an ideal material for boat hulls, skis, storage tanks, automobile parts, and hundreds of other applications. For twenty-five years, as the basic fiberglass product was gradually improved, a variety of industries found an increasing number of uses for the material, and PPG's Reinforced Plastics Group expanded steadily.

The Reinforced Plastic Group's environment was typical of those enjoyed by companies with a dominant position in a healthy, growing, commodity-type market. It was able to sell just about as much of its relatively standard products as it could produce.

The key to success in this growing marketplace was an outstanding manufacturing operation that was able to produce high-quality products at competitive prices. The group's other functions, although competently run and successful, had less critical roles to play in growth and profitability than did manufacturing. Sales representatives called on customers, many of whom were already committed to PPG's product. Marketing made forecasts, established pricing, and set sales priorities. The technical people solved quality problems and searched for product innovations that would give PPG an additional competitive edge. With manufacturing leading the parade, each function performed its tasks according to its own priorities and goals, and there was little need for collaboration across the entire business.

>> PPG Fiber Glass Products

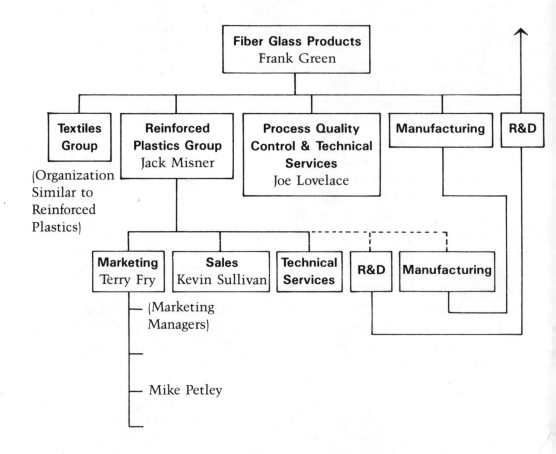

It was a successful pattern of operations. If the marketplace had not changed, that pattern could have gone on indefinitely.

The String Runs Out

By the early 1980s, when the Reinforced Plastics Group had passed the $200-million level, several trends surfaced in the marketplace. First, so many inventive uses for fiberglass-reinforced plastics had been developed over the years that the group was running out of new opportunities. As a result of this trend, and of a leveling off of sales in some of their best product lines, the prime customers of the Reinforced Plastics Group began to experience a decline in their rate of expansion. At the same time, imported fiberglass at lower selling prices began to appear. What had been a marketplace with room for everyone to be profitable quickly became highly competitive. With margins and the rate of growth falling, the managers realized that their business was in some danger. That fact was underlined when the corporation downgraded the group's strategic rating—meaning that only limited capital funding would be available to the Reinforced Plastics Group.

To find new applications that would revitalize their businesses, the plastics manufacturers—who were PPG's customers—began experimenting successfully with new compositions of fiberglass with unique characteristics. It was clear that PPG's growth opportunities in the future would depend on its ability to tailor its fiberglass to meet specific, shifting customer needs. What had been a market for a commodity product was now going to demand proficiency in customer responsiveness and adaptability.

It was clear that reestablishing themselves as a growth business was not going to be a matter merely of cutting costs, hiring some new people, or getting everyone to work harder. The Reinforced Plastics Group would have to become a fundamentally different type of organization. It had been geared to the gradual improvement of existing products. Now it would have to learn to develop new products rapidly and creatively. Its high-volume production system was geared to standard products. Now it would have to learn to meet changing customer requirements. The central role of manufacturing, with support roles for the other functions, would have to be transformed into close, active, unified collaboration among all of the functions.

A tall order.

Formulating a Strategy

Green's dilemma was how to get the Reinforced Plastics organization, with its deeply ingrained work habits, moving in this new direction. He knew that any large-scale management development or "culture change" program or reorganization would do no more than divert energy. He had a number of good people who he thought were capable of providing the leadership for the transformation—although he knew it would require of them a tremendous amount of personal change and development. He decided that the breakthrough strategy would be useful for working with these people, one step at a time, to completely transform the old PPG Reinforced Plastics Group—without missing a beat along the way.

His idea for getting started was to select a critical product family or market area; have his people make some immediate progress in expanding the business in that area; and simultaneously test the three major organizational shifts that he thought were necessary:

1. establishing the marketing managers as the true leaders for each product line;
2. increasing the capacity of the functional areas to rapidly create a unified response to identified market opportunities; and
3. significantly accelerating the pace of new product development.

Selecting an Area of Focus

With these goals in mind, and knowing that he was setting out on a difficult voyage, Frank Green took a deep breath and got started.

He convened a meeting of the top functional managers for Reinforced Plastics to officially launch the transformation process. He described his view of the severity of the marketplace shift: "We have no choice. Survival requires that we learn how to respond much faster and much more effectively to changing customer needs."

After they had been introduced to the results-centered concepts of the breakthrough strategy, he told his managers that he wanted them to decide on the best place to begin. He asked them to select a product family for which PPG was not capturing its share of the market, and for which some strenuous efforts to innovate might be rewarded with significant gains.

This was the first time that the top functional managers of Reinforced Plastics had sat down together to work on a common goal. They had always come to meetings more as delegates from their own functions than as members of a management team. "I was amazed at the diversity of opinion about what the goal should be," recalled Joe Lovelace, the manager of Process Quality Control and Technical Services. "Each of us was struggling over how difficult it would be for our own functions to do what might have to be done—rather than looking at what we all wanted to achieve from an overall business perspective."

The managers agreed that the "direct chop" process was the place to focus. This process cuts fiberglass into very short lengths used to reinforce plastic products. It was an area with considerable promise, but they had not yet been able to respond with competitive products. PPG was selling nothing at all to one of the largest users of the material, and was not participating in the fastest growing, high-margin segment of the market. The poor performance of the chopped-strand product line was dragging down the overall results of the Reinforced Plastics Group.

To provide a sense of direction, the managers decided that it would be useful to define an overall goal for their effort. They agreed—after a grueling three-hour debate—that over the next three years they would develop three new chopped-strand products and sell them to at least six major customers, with a combined sales volume of 800,000 pounds per month, at a specified profit margin. This group had taken its first step into the new era.

Launching the First Breakthrough

The next step was to take this ambitious long-term goal and find within it a few short-term goals. It was made clear that the breakthrough projects had to help the marketing managers make the big shift into leadership roles in making Reinforced Plastics more customer-focused. Previously, the narrowly defined administrative roles of the marketing managers had never included this level of responsibility.

Mike Petley, the marketing manager for chopped-strand products, was selected as the leader of the first project team.

When he learned that he would be coordinating the efforts of people he did not have authority over, he was very uncomfortable. He was too familiar with how each function operated, and he knew they would not change easily. "The good relations I've developed over the years are important to me," he said. "I can't start telling people what to do and when to do it."

Nevertheless, he assembled a breakthrough team that started with the overall goal defined by the management group and then came up with a one-year goal for the sales of two chopped-strand products. Next, they established a ninety-day action plan with coordinated subgoals for each of the functional areas, such as running tests on specific technical processes, identifying cost reduction alternatives, and establishing contacts with certain customers.

The next challenge was to build the participation of the functions. Manufacturing performance was measured on volume and cost variances; experimenting with new products would slow that department's output and undermine its cost reduction efforts. A conflict loomed between a traditional functional goal and a new organizational goal. The team responded to these concerns. Working together with the department, they devised ways to minimize the disruptive impact on Manufacturing of testing new produts.

The R&D department also seemed reluctant. Petley's view had been: "Our project work is not very glamorous, and so it's hard to get their attention. They prefer to concentrate on exciting new technologies." When he talked with a scientist from R&D, however, he was told, "You don't get us the information clearly, and the messages keep changing, so we concentrate on other work. If you would tell us specifically what you really need, we could design the product."

The truth struck home. In the past, the marketing managers had not been able to give R&D enough guidance because they and the salespeople rarely developed really clear understandings about customer needs. With the help of its representative from R&D, the breakthrough team established much sharper priorities for the project's R&D work. From that point on, the marketing and R&D team members worked in regular collaboration on developing new products.

As a result of their interfunctional collaboration on the project—and of the revelation that properly exercised leadership by a marketing manager would actually be welcomed, not challenged—the breakthrough team was beginning to find out how to operate in the new mode. They were, in effect, designing their own "culture-change program."

By April of 1985, six months after the project had begun, the team had successfully coordinated and accomplished a series of their short-term goals. Although they still had a long way to go, progress was coming more under their control.

New Effectiveness in the Marketplace

The breakthrough team was demonstrating how to build closer relationships with customers, how to speed up new product development, and how to collaborate as an interfunctional team. The experiment seemed to be working so well that Jack Misner, the general manager of Reinforced Plastics, decided to get his other five marketing managers to lead breakthrough projects.

One of these teams, headed by marketing manager Rich Alexander, began working with an automotive parts manufacturer. This customer was developing a reinforced-plastic suspension spring for one of the major automobile companies. Although it was originally intended for use only on one particular model, the team recognized that there was an opportunity to enter a much broader market.

To begin, the team identified one technical breakthrough project: solving a specific problem the customer was experiencing. That success, achieved fairly quickly, demonstrated their commitment to the customer and their capacity to help. As they continued to work on the product's development, however, they ran into a serious roadblock: working separately, the PPG team (which was improving the characteristics of the fiberglass) and the customer (who was developing the proprietary process by which the fiberglass was bonded to the plastic materials) were unable to identify the reasons for failures. Because they had already won the trust and confidence of the customer, the PPG team was able to reach an unusual agreement. The customer would help recreate the highly confidential proprietary process within PPG. Being able to work in customer-simulated conditions enabled the teams to solve the problems together. One team member explained, "We actually included the customer's people in our work plans. They had to meet jointly set deadlines so that we could continue our development work. They understood that they were part of the team."

The result was a new application for fiberglass, which later expanded beyond the one model originally targeted. Moreover, the project built the customer's commitment to PPG as their sole supplier of fiberglass. Project by project, the marketing managers and their teams were discovering for themselves how to compete and succeed in the new fiberglass marketplace. What they were learning from this project would stay with them through their entire careers.

Sales Management Gets into the Act

The broad strategic shifts occurring within Reinforced Plastics required changes within the sales force. No longer was it enough for salespeople to go to customers and ask for orders out of a catalogue of fairly standard products. They had to find out what was going on in the customer's business and work closely with the customer. They had to be on the lookout for new opportunities and to alert Marketing whenever they spotted one. They had to become a source of market intelligence.

To begin this transformation, the director of sales, Kevin Sullivan, introduced a new sales management system. Together with his territory managers and their salespeople, he developed a series of short-term sales goals to focus energy on the most important existing and target accounts.

To achieve these zestful short-term goals, Sullivan encouraged his sales representatives to try testing some innovative steps. In the past, they had never set prices or negotiated contracts. Now, as a test, one salesman was given a range for pricing and the terms within which he could negotiate. He handled the proceedings himself and was able to win 100 percent of one customer's business for the year at a price that was comfortably above the minimum allowable.

In an effort to win a new account, another salesman developed a proposal for PPG to work with the customer in developing and testing a new material. The president of the customer company was reluctant to commit his people and resources to help PPG develop a product. The salesman suggested a small, first-step effort that required only a little customer involvement, but that could pay some real dividends. He won his point, and a start was made. Success on the first step has led to a continuing growth on that account ever since.

In another case, a sales representative, with the help of marketing and technical people, was able to help a customer adapt a standard product to some unique applications. He was then able to negotiate a price premium that made the product one of the most profitable in the line.

In each of these cases, the sales people were taking on a level of responsibility they had never assumed before. They were experimenting with new ways to work with customers, and they were asking for and receiving help from the other functions. More and more, the different functions within Reinforced Plastics were jointly working toward shared business goals.

Helping to Make PPG's Distributors More Successful

These early successes of his sales group encouraged the director to attempt a bold experiment. Although his own sales force was getting closer to their customers, much of PPG's fiberglass was sold indirectly through a network of distributors. The only way to do a better job with those customers was by strengthening the selling and managerial skills of the distributors.

This required a profound shift in approach for PPG's sales people. Before, they had been simply "pushing product" to their distributors; now they were going to try to be teachers and consultants. Starting with a few distributors who seemed most open to collaboration, the PPG representatives ran some goal-setting and work-planning sessions aimed at helping their distributors get a greater return on time invested in selling PPG products. They scheduled formal follow-up quarterly reviews in which, together, they would evaluate progress and see what further support the distributors might need.

Here's one illustration of the benefit of this process: PPG identified one low-performing distributor who had always been concerned that sales of its own line of products would suffer if it focused on other products. The sessions with the PPG representatives helped this distributor see how to increase its own current sales while expanding its attention to other products. In one year, this distributor tripled its sales of fiberglass and became one of the top ten PPG fiberglass distributors.

A Multiplication Strategy Is Created

During the first year, each project was launched as a fresh undertaking. As momentum increased, however, Misner decided to try to accelerate the process. A number of new tools and mechanisms were created to institutionalize the breakthrough strategy and to spread knowledge and skill more easily. For example, a guidebook was developed to outline the role of the project manager and to help new teams—which they called Program Management Teams—benefit from the successful experiences of the early teams.

Terry Fry, the director of marketing for Reinforced Plastics—and the person to whom the marketing managers reported—took on the role of breakthrough facilitator, not only for his own group but for the Textiles Group, the other business within PPG's Fiber Glass Products. As one of his projects, he developed a videotape that has been used to publicize and gain support for further expansion of the breakthrough strategy within the entire division.

The Expansion Moves Across Business Lines

In order to stimulate interest in the Textiles Group, Terry Fry invited his counterpart, John Musser, that group's marketing director, to attend a series of discussions summarizing the experience of the project leaders in Reinforced Plastics. Impressed by what he heard and by the results of the projects, Musser decided to get a team started in Textiles.

The first project team began to work on a fiberglass yarn used to make printed circuit boards. The team decided on an ambitious goal: they would attempt to double the market penetration of this one product. Following the lead of the Reinforced Plastics teams, they went directly to the customer to find out what they needed to work on. They were surprised by how readily they were able to identify several key customer requirements. Responding to those necessitated some not-too-difficult improvements in the product's chemistry, in quality control, and in the packaging of the yarn. They were able to make all of these changes, and the success of this project led to the formation of other teams within the Textiles Group; the expansion of the breakthrough strategy continued.

A New Top-Management Team Emerges

When they originally came together to launch the direct chop breakthrough project, the top managers of Reinforced Plastics were really individuals preoccupied with the concerns of their own functions. Gradually, they coalesced into an effective steering group. As they continued to work together over several years—launching breakthrough projects, bringing functions together, resolving disputes, and allocating resources—they began to see themselves as the comanagers of a single business. It was a radical change wrought by a tremendous amount of hard work, give-and-take, and shared success.

With operational and marketing tasks coming under greater control, and with their confidence rising in their fellow managers throughout Reinforced Plastics, this steering committee now had the opportunity to focus on longer term planning. In the past, without a genuine team effort, planning had always been a rather bureaucratic exercise. Plans were dutifully submitted to top management, but had little practical influence on functional priorities or managerial work patterns. Now they had the time and the perspective to develop shared creative strategies. And they translated those strategies into action steps. They defined the responsibilities of each function and made sure there would be a project team to work on every single key goal.

Putting It All Together

Step by step, project by project, over the last several years the Reinforced Plastics Group has become, with the very same people, an entirely new organization. The marketing managers have learned to play a lead role. The sales representatives are actively building account relationships and supporting their distributors. All of the functions are working together to further reduce costs, maintain quality, and respond to new product requirements. And a top-management team has emerged to lead the process.

The bottom-line results tell the story: the domestic market share of the Reinforced Plastics Group has now reached an all-time high and is continuing to grow. As the group has shown improved results, the corporation has upgraded its strategic rating from "cash cow" to "high-growth business."

With this reevaluation, PPG Industries gave Fiber Glass Products the approval and the resources to expand. Its management team is now busy investigating and developing new opportunities in world markets for their revitalized division. Recently, they signed agreements for joint ventures in Taiwan and Venezuela and completed the acquisition of a company in Great Britain. Teams are using the breakthrough strategy approaches to plan and carry out the integration of these overseas ventures into a global enterprise.

>> Top Management's New Job

While I have concentrated in this book on describing the "building blocks" of the breakthrough strategy, the success of the Fiber Glass team—and that of others like them—shows that it is top management that must "shape the cathedral" from the well-carved stones of individual projects. As the architects of the overall change process, top management needs to orchestrate five key tasks.

1. Establish the context and the challenge.
When PPG's Fiber Glass vice president showed his people the shifts that had occurred in their environment and helped them to see that their current mode of operation would, if not changed, make it impossible to cope with new demands, and in addition, laid out a practical plan for responding to the challenges, he was doing the single most critical task of any top executive.

That task is to shape a clear and compelling definition of what the organization must do to be successful. The senior executive must interpret the events and trends that affect his or her business and make sure that steps are set in motion to respond to them.

2. Set increasingly tough demands as performance capacity grows.
Senior management must be certain that every unit in the company has translated its large, far-reaching performance improvement targets into breakthrough goals. No unit of the organization should be exempt from the requirement to be perpetually working on an array of short-term projects with clear-cut goals that require constant experimentation with better ways to get the job done.

3. Test new directions through strategic breakthrough projects.
Senior management must make sure that every part of the organization is actively experimenting with pilot projects that lead in new strategic directions. The idea must take root that strategy does not consist only of a few big decisions, but also of many small decisions, experiments—and actions.

4. Make technology support performance improvement.
Top management must ensure that technical specialists introduce innovations in a way that directly supports the attainment of goals that users in the organization are striving to achieve. Technological innovators must be helped to see themselves as consultants, supporters, and facilitators of organization change.

5. Orchestrate the total program of progress.
The orchestration of all of the individual activities is the last element of the architecture of change. It is not enough to have your twenty or fifty or five hundred individual strands of progress. It is top management's task to braid the elements together and to be able to present a total picture of progress to the rest of the organization, showing how all the elements support each other.

» *A Learning Environment*

The whole corporate development process needs to take place in an environment in which it is clear that everybody is learning together, including top management. Many corporate change projects are launched and managed with the implication that top management is in possession of final answers, and that if the rest of the organization would just do its part, everything would fall into place.

The breakthrough strategy conveys the idea that top management will be learning from the rest of the organization while the organization will be learning from top management. Bob Galvin emphasized this point when he launched Motorola's "Organization Effectiveness Process" and invited every manager in the corporation to share the task with him: "The conclusion of our effort cannot be precisely defined now. To define it is the purpose of launching this exercise. . ."

Yes, if American industry is really going to compete successfully, there is no doubt that many changes, on many different levels, must be made. The place to start, however, is within your own organization.

You can begin today. You will be able to see results, not in months or years, but in weeks. As soon as you finish reading this page, write down the few most important improvements that would make your organization (or your part of it) more competitive. Then identify some short-term steps that you can take toward those goals—steps that you can achieve with the resources you already have, with a minimum of preliminaries, and without waiting for everyone else to do their part of the job.

And then. . .well, you know what comes next. Good luck!

>> About the Author

Robert H. Schaffer earned both a bachelor's degree in mechanical engineering and a doctorate in management psychology from Columbia University. After several teaching and research assignments, he entered the management consulting field. Within a few years he launched the firm of Robert H. Schaffer & Associates and has headed it ever since. The firm employs the breakthrough strategy in helping companies and other kinds of organizations to achieve short-term performance gains while strengthening their capacity to achieve longer term, more ambitious strategic goals. Mr. Schaffer and his colleagues often collaborate with and train internal staff and consultants as a key dimension of their work with large organizations.

Schaffer has been active in the management consulting profession. He was a founding director of the Institute of Management Consultants and was chairman of its professional development committee for a number of years. Currently he serves as an editor of the *Journal of Management Consulting*.

Although this is his first book, Schaffer has written many articles, including four that have appeared in the *Harvard Business Review*. He lives in Stamford, Connecticut, and divides his time between his firm's operations there and in Toronto.

If you are interested in how you might exploit the breakthrough strategy in your own organization, you can contact the author or his colleagues in Robert H. Schaffer & Associates at 401 Rockrimmon Road, Stamford, Connecticut 06903 (203-322-1604). In Canada, the address is 67 Yonge Street, Suite 1400, Toronto, Ontario M5E 1J8 (416-864-9488). Support can be provided both to managers who want to employ the approach in their organizations and to staff specialists who want to use the approach with their clients within their organizations.